AF712654

LIVING WELL, SAVING FOR LIFE

Living Well, Saving for Life

A Guide for Creating Wealth on a Modest Income

BY

NEIL CHODOROW

Stone Quail
PRESS

Cover and interior design by Masha Shubin, Inkwater Press®
The growth of the tree © violetkaipa. BigStockPhoto.com

Chodorow, Neil.
Living well, saving for life : a guide for creating wealth on a modest income / by Neil Chodorow.
pages cm
LCCN 2015904459
ISBN-13: 978-0-9909474-0-0 (paperback)
ISBN-10: 0-9909474-0-8 (paperback)
ISBN-13: 978-0-9909474-1-7 (Kindle)
ISBN-10: 0-9909474-1-6 (Kindle)

1. Finance, Personal. 2. Wealth. I. Title.

HG179.C5557 2015 332.024'01
QBI15-361

Publisher: Stone Quail Press | www.stonequailpress.com

Paperback ISBN-13 978-0-9909474-0-0 | ISBN-10 0-9909474-0-8
Kindle ISBN-13 978-0-9909474-1-7 | ISBN-10 0-9909474-1-6

Printed in the U.S.A.

1 3 5 7 9 10 8 6 4 2

This book is dedicated to my wife, Susie, for her encouragement and valuable suggestions. And to our sons, Nick and Josh, along with others in their generation, in the hopes they will be able to retire with security and dignity when they reach my age.

TABLE OF CONTENTS

PART 2

SAVING FOR LIFE

LIST OF CHARTS

PREFACE

THIS BOOK WAS INSPIRED BY THE WEALTHY BARBER BY DAVID CHILTON, a wildly popular and humorous 1984 Canadian book about personal financial planning my wife and I used when we were younger. When I reread the book recently at my wife's suggestion, I realized how much great information it contained for people with modest incomes who wish to create wealth for themselves and their families. But I also realized that much of the book's information about taxes, real estate, and return on investments was hopelessly outdated.

In addition, Chilton's advice was specific to Canada and did not translate well to the situation faced by Americans, then or now. For example, Canadians receive universal health insurance from their government, paid for by income taxes. So Chilton omits any mention of health costs as a factor in a family's budgeting or financial planning. And since even elite private Canadian colleges and universities are inexpensive by American standards, there is little discussion about saving or paying for education. Lastly, property-based taxes are not used in Canada to support public schools. So decisions about where to live within the same province are not driven by severe school funding and local taxation disparities.

I am intimately familiar with these differences. My wife and I spent our early adulthood and began our retirement planning as visual artists living in rural Prince Edward Island, Canada. Then we completed it in a suburb of Rochester NY, USA, where I retired as an elementary school teacher in 2009, just before my 63rd birthday.

Throughout this process, my wife and I learned how to live on a modest income and save for retirement, developing the skills needed to create and monitor a financial plan for ourselves. As a result, we have entered retirement with a feeling of financial security and comfort.

As our discussions about Chilton's book continued, my wife suggested I write a book for young Americans that would focus on the lessons I had learned. Once I decided to do so, I studied other books of this type. Among them, I was most struck by Smart Money Moves For African Americans, written by Kelvin Boston in 1996. This excellent book has a dual purpose. First, Boston outlines the economic actions the African American population as a whole needs to take to create community-wide prosperity. Second, he suggests lifestyle and financial steps African American families should take to attain enough wealth to secure their own futures.

Reading Boston's book 15 years after its publication raised some disturbing issues. According to the 2010 census, the lack of household wealth Boston described among most African Americans has grown worse. Meanwhile, the long-term debt African Americans had in 1996 now applies more generally to the entire American working and middle classes. If this trend continues, we may sadly reach a new economic "equality" in which a large percentage of all Americans are poor and devoid of the skills needed to change their poverty. In fact, in 2002 my older brother presciently called the impending disappearance of the American middle class "the Latin America-fication" of the United States.

Given these developments, I decided my updated and "Americanized" version of Chilton's book should include Boston's focus on understanding key economic concepts and lifestyle choices that will affect young Americans' financial wellbeing years from now. I also hoped the tone of my book, although unfortunately lacking Chilton's humor, would offer a sense of encouragement and hope to young people who are constantly being told there is nothing but economic gloom and doom ahead.

For those who like to see "data" behind financial suggestions, I have followed Boston's example by including brief mathematical discussions and charts. But don't worry. The wealth-building steps recommended here do not require special financial or mathematical expertise.

Some examples in this book use specific dollar amounts, which are rounded to the nearest $5. The numbers in these examples are only meant to illustrate the concepts under discussion. None are meant to match *your* financial situation. And none match mine. Lastly, key terms and ideas throughout the text appear in italics for extra emphasis, while the book ends with a Glossary that defines key words and phrases in the text.

INTRODUCTION

QUESTIONS AND ANSWERS

RECENTLY, MY WIFE AND I HAVE BEEN ANSWERING A LOT OF QUESTIONS from younger adults about personal financial matters. "What is an IRA?" "What are the differences among 401(k) plans, 403Bs, regular IRAs, SEP-IRAs, and Roth IRAs?" "What kind of mortgage should I get?" "What should I do about life, disability, or long-term care insurance?" "How do I decide how much house I can *really* afford?" "How should I save for my children's education, or pay for it when they are in college or after graduation?" "How much should I save each year?" "How does Social Security work?" And, "how can anyone who isn't already rich save money?" The list goes on and on.

Even some of our older acquaintances have asked questions, primarily about distributions from retirement funds, investment strategies, retirement housing choices, or the merits and risks of long-term care insurance, annuities, and reverse mortgages.

While I enjoy answering these questions, doing so has raised a concern about the lack of financial knowledge and confidence possessed by many Americans today. While it is important to avoid judging anyone else's lifestyle or financial choices, the frequency of these questions makes it clear a lot of young and not-so-young Americans need help understanding how to evaluate the lifestyle options they have and how the choices they *do* make will affect their financial future.

Rather than continuing to answer these questions in isolation, which always gives me the urge to explain something else connected to the topic at hand (the curse of all teachers), I decided to take my wife's advice and write a book about the *lifestyle and financial topics* of spending, inflation, saving, compound interest, investing, insurance, education, homeownership, mortgages, consumer debt, and taxes. Along the way, I would touch on the long-term consequences of choices available in each of these areas. Then, the last and shorter section of my book would focus on creating a financial plan for before *and* after retirement. Given the range of people's values and goals, there are many right ways to do this. However, this section is based on the belief that having a financial plan that fits *your* values and goals is right for everyone, especially those with modest incomes.

✦

The need for this kind of information has never been more urgent. Despite living in what has recently been called a terrible economic time, my generation will have more wealth in old age than any earlier American generation. And this wealth will have to be managed and sustained. For younger Americans there are additional issues, including greater uncertainty about old-age programs like Social Security and Medicare; the disappearance and erosion of pensions and other retirement benefits; and governments and employers withdrawing from the "parental" role of managing the funds that have traditionally provided security for retired Americans.

Given these changes in our economy and culture, it is clear Americans will have to develop the skills needed to accumulate wealth during their working years. It is equally clear that more and more ill-prepared Americans will soon find themselves in the uncomfortable position of having to manage their own finances, both before and after retirement.

The four key questions associated with the need for wealth and financial management skills are:

- How can you save money and accumulate wealth during your working years?
- How can you decide how much wealth you will need and therefore the pace at which you should save for retirement?
- How can you grow your savings until retirement?
- How should you use your wealth in retirement to ensure "the money outlasts you" or is available for other goals?

We will look at all these questions. Each chapter is framed by real questions my wife and I have been asked. While my advice is the opposite of a "get rich quick scheme," if you follow the steps outlined in this book you will develop the habits needed to amass enough wealth to maintain a good lifestyle until the end of your life. However, before describing the actions you should take to reach this financial goal we must begin by taking a short detour to define "wealth," a much misunderstood and politically abused term in America today.

PART 1

LIVING WELL

CHAPTER 1

WHAT IS WEALTH?

An Overview of Topics to Come

PERHAPS THE MOST IMPORTANT LESSON I HAVE LEARNED THROUGH MANaging my own finances and discussing financial matters with others is there is no set amount of assets or income that makes someone wealthy. Despite what many people think, being a "millionaire," winning the lottery, or making a yearly income over $150,000 does not guarantee someone is or will remain wealthy. Or that they will *feel* wealthy. Instead, the only meaningful definition of wealth is *you* having enough money to live the way you want to live, now and in the future. For example, if you are currently living happily on a gross (total before taxes) *household* income of $80,000 per year, wealth should be defined as earning enough to sustain your lifestyle during your working years and then having enough assets and income to continue that lifestyle in retirement.

Like Goldilocks and the Three Bears, $80,000 in today's dollars may be "just right" for one family but unimaginable wealth or abject poverty for others. For a family living on $55,000, having an income of $80,000 might feel like "winning the Lottery." In fact, having an extra $25,000 per year for life *is* roughly equivalent to getting an after-tax Lottery winning of $500,000. However, for someone living on an income of $110,000 or more, an $80,000 income might feel like poverty.

Of course, many people would say a family with a lower future income should just "tighten their belts" and learn to live a more modest lifestyle. Within limits, this is true. Many people could live on a little less without being any less happy once they did so. But it is important to acknowledge that the income needs of families are not comparable or fully adjustable. This is true for six reasons that, taken together, are the keys to defining wealth for *your* family.

LOCATION, LOCATION, LOCATION

Where you live greatly affects *housing costs* and therefore the need for income. For example, a nice middle-class house in an Upstate New York city or rural "exurb" can be had for $100,000. But a similar house in other cities and desirable resort, weekend, and summer home locations might cost $500,000 to $1,000,000 or even more.

Once you buy a home, there is the cost of ownership. School and property taxes in one place can be five times the taxes on a similar house in another place. And maintaining or renovating a home is more costly in expensive housing areas. Nevertheless, in most local areas there are urban, suburban, and rural options with different levels of prestige and price profiles. So, buying a home that fits your budget is sometimes about making choices available in your region's housing market. However, it remains true that *a reasonable house purchase in one community may be much more expensive than in another community*.

Finally, most Americans believe owning a home is an essential part of "the American Dream." But if homes are too expensive for your budget in your area, it makes sense to rent. You should also rent if you expect to relocate soon. There are two reasons for this. First, you may have to do expensive repairs without spreading out those costs over many years of use of the home. And second, the tax advantages of ownership do not outweigh the upfront costs until you have owned a home for at least five years. Of course, the availability and cost of rental homes and apartments play a large role in the "renting versus owning" choice. Communities with high rates of homeownership are also more stable and attractive. So owning a home contributes to the environment in which most people would like to live. But it is important to remember that renters can also have full adult lives and save for retirement.

HEALTH

Ben Franklin said it is self-evident being "healthy, wealthy, and wise" is valuable for everyone. But given the cost of American *health care* today, we should probably add "having *health insurance*" to his list. Two families can have vastly different income needs solely based on the health of family members, access to health insurance, or out-of-pocket health care costs. According to the Insurance Council of America, the cost of health insurance in the United States has increased at a rate more than double the rate of inflation over the last 20 years. To make matters worse, employer contributions to health insurance premiums have been cut, a trend certain to continue with or without changes to our health care system associated with the Affordable Care Act of 2010. As a result, out-of-pocket costs are rising, even for those *with* insurance. Meanwhile, uninsured individuals pay more to hospitals and health care providers than insurance companies, who as mass purchasers of medical services pay a "discounted" price. So those without insurance face a double whammy: higher bills *and* sole responsibility for paying them. Not surprisingly, Americans who have inadequate, overly expensive, or no health insurance coverage have difficulty keeping up with their other bills or saving for the future.

THE TWO UNSPOKEN R'S OF EDUCATION: RESUMES AND REPAYMENT

Many parents preach to their children about the value of a college education, but have no idea how to pay for it. Meanwhile, few adults recognize the high cost of pre-college (K-12) education or the need to save for additional education for themselves. One thing, however, is clear: as our economy changes, a quality education with a good credential attached is becoming more important in defining who succeeds in America. This may not be fair, but it is how our society works.

Unfortunately, as the value of education has increased so has the cost, at a pace that, like health care, has far outstripped inflation. *Your* education costs, of course, depend on the size of your family, the local availability of high-quality public K-12 education, your or your children's scholarship-worthiness, and the post-secondary choices in your state or region. Lastly, paying back student loans *after* an education is done is a substantial financial burden for many families and former students. So paying for education entails grossly different investments in different families.

FINANCIAL RESPONSIBILITIES FOR OTHERS

No two families are alike. Some have no children, others have two, and some have far more. Some couples have children when they are in their 20s, while others do so in their 30s or early 40s. An increasing number of families have children with special needs requiring costly treatments when young and continuing care in adulthood. Many parents and grandparents provide financial help to children or grandchildren, not only during the traditional "childhood years" but also as they get an education or haltingly move toward full adulthood. Even paying for a child's wedding may derail a family's savings plan or plunge parents into debt. And lastly, some families are financially responsible for elderly parents. Those responsible for children and parents at the same time are called the "sandwich generation." In a clever variant of this term, a recent report on National Public Radio about people financially responsible for grandchildren, children *and* parents all at the same time called these people the "club sandwich generation." Moreover, the differences among families in relation to these responsibilities can create very different needs for assets and income, now and in the future.

ENTREPRENEURSHIP: THE BUSINESS OF SMALL BUSINESS

Some people own businesses or income-producing properties. This is more than a way to earn a living. These assets may grow in value, be sold later, or handed down to the next generation, generating income for retirement or an inheritance for heirs. The risks and rewards of creating wealth in this way lie beyond the scope of this book. However, people who invest personal savings or company profits in a business are saving for their future. While their need to separately save for retirement may therefore be less than for others, business owners should have other investments in case the business falters or it becomes necessary to sell it at a bad time due to illness, death, or other causes. It is also important to legally separate family and personal property, home, and savings from a business so they are not lost if the business goes into bankruptcy or is sued.

BENEFITS: THE LUCK OF THE DRAW

People receive *benefits* of vastly different value from employers, family, or friends. Some employers pay some or all health insurance and education costs. Some employees retain health insurance benefits after retirement, while others who received this benefit when working must pay for health insurance or a much greater share of it once they retire. Some employers contribute to employees' retirement funds while others do not. Some employers provide pensions while others do not. Meanwhile, some families can call on financial assistance from family or friends to cover basic expenses, pay off debts, or buy a house or other big ticket item.

When it comes to creating wealth, it does not matter whether these benefits come from an employer, friend, or family member. Having them eases a family's income needs, making saving for retirement easier. If this disparity continues into retirement, this one factor may make a huge difference in the level of savings a family will need.

✦

In summary, it is not fair to say anyone who requires more income than you is "spoiled" or over-spending. Or anyone living on less is doomed to poverty. Remember, wealth for one person is not wealth for everyone. Your goal should simply be to accumulate enough assets and benefits to sustain your lifestyle until the end of your and your spouse's or partner's lives, or, if you want, to have enough assets to leave some wealth to heirs or charities. As with much else in life, it is best to concentrate on your own situation without judging the behavior of others. Nor does it make sense to think ill or well of your own life and wealth by comparing yourself to others.

CHAPTER 2

SPENDING VERSUS EARNING

Question: How can we save money when we always seem to spend more than we earn?

Despite the flexible definition of wealth in Chapter 1, for those in the middle class *attaining wealth is more dependent on spending than it is on the amount of income earned*. The key is to make *lifestyle* choices that allow you to *"live below your means"* and put money aside for later, no matter what your income. Or, to invert an old saying, "spend money like there *is* a tomorrow."

According to the 2010 census, 48% of American households make $45,000 or less per year. For this segment of society, it is virtually impossible to provide for the necessities of life *and* save for the future, especially in high-cost locations in America. Given these numbers, *households with "modest" incomes will be defined throughout this book as those with gross incomes from $50,000 to $110,000*. We will develop financial plans across this range of incomes. But we will use the average of these limits, *$80,000*, in many examples in later chapters.

Unfortunately, Americans at every income level are constantly encouraged to spend beyond their means. If we get an inheritance, pay raise, bonus, tax rebate or cut, or win the lottery, we buy a bigger house or car, go on a better vacation, or become more "elite" consumers. So *our lifestyle expands whenever our income does*. Moreover, few Americans treat increased income as a benefit to be put aside for the future. As a result, when a family's income declines, usually due to a lay-off, divorce, or ill health, having made a good income does not guarantee economic security.

The negative consequences of these American spending habits are getting worse with each passing year. In the late-1980s, *individual* after-inflation incomes declined for the first time since the 1930s while wealth was concentrated in fewer hands, reaching a level of inequality never previously seen in America. By 2012, the wealthiest 1% of American households had the same wealth as the poorest 90%! This wealth gap has been widely discussed in relation to race and gender. But the gap between households headed by someone over 65 and those headed by someone under 35 has also grown and been ignored. In 1985, the average older household had 10 times the wealth of an average younger one, an understandable difference given the accumulation of assets throughout life. However, by 2012, *older families had 47 times the wealth of younger ones*, a ratio that clearly reflects the shrinkage of the middle class and the failure of young Americans to save for the future.

In the 1990s, the drop in inflation-adjusted individual incomes was hidden by the number of women who entered the workforce. As a result, many families had two breadwinners for the first time and household incomes continued to rise, fueling more lavish lifestyles. However, by 2000, the infusion of new second incomes leveled off. Unfortunately, despite a drop in inflation-adjusted *household* income, many families kept on spending, in large part fueled by long-term debt.

In addition, a household that is *not* spending a lot of money is often described as being downright unpatriotic. After all, consumer spending for goods and services now makes up roughly 90% of the American economy, a fact that, by itself, is unhealthy for our economic future. So, while "savers" are protecting their own families' futures, they are supposedly "hurting" our current economy.

Even governments promote this way of thinking. Whenever a local, state, or the federal government reduces taxes or gives taxpayers a tax rebate, it is trumpeted as a way to increase consumer spending, which will stimulate businesses and job creation. It is never pointed out that *saved* money is usually invested, thereby stimulating the American economy in a more structural and sustainable way.

Despite these pressures, *saving money is just as sensible today as it was 100 years ago.* There is also room for *thriftiness* in every lifestyle. To cite one example, in 2005 I taught a unit on division, decimal fractions, and averages to a group of 5th Grade students by focusing on economic "need" versus "want." In a survey of 100 students' homes in our middle-class community, we discovered the average family had 5.7 televisions and 4.4 people. In 2005, I believed that having a television was a necessity. But having more than one per person, not to mention the vast array of other entertainment systems in students' homes, was clearly a want not a need. Moreover, when students listed all the appliances, gadgets, and systems that ran on electricity in their homes as part of the same project, the results led, I was told, to some very interesting discussions around kitchen tables about *moderation*.

As this project demonstrated, some expenses could be trimmed and still leave needs fulfilled. While the savings gained from this "trimming" might be minor for some families, looking at all purchases through a lens of *need versus want* and *comparative shopping* for all goods and services to get the best price and product would add up to a significant saving for everyone, in every lifestyle and at every income level.

Lastly, among the most important aspects of thriftiness is the role of borrowing versus saving. We will look at this topic in detail in later chapters. For now it is worth emphasizing that in general *the less you borrow, especially for wants, the wealthier you will become over time. And, equally, the more you save and invest your savings, the wealthier you will become.*

CHAPTER 3

HANDLING WEALTH AS YOU CREATE IT

Questions: What should I do with money I save? How do I keep from using up all my savings in emergencies? Won't I end up with enough wealth in the value of my house?

NO MATTER HOW WELL YOU CONTROL YOUR SPENDING OR HOW CONSISTENTLY you save there are two "money management" principles that are essential to creating wealth.

"PARK" YOUR MONEY IN "DRIVE" SO IT WORKS FOR YOU

There's an old saying that goes, "money makes money." This makes it sound as if you already have to be rich to end up wealthy. However, for those with modest incomes, it is more accurate to say "*you make money and save some of it. Then your saved money makes wealth.*"

Where can you put saved money so it will create wealth? Luckily, there are investment accounts designed to house money for retirement. Most of them assess penalties for withdrawals before reaching age 59½. This is a good thing because these penalties keep people from raiding their retirement accounts, which makes them more effective savings "locked boxes." Nevertheless, to avoid *having* to borrow from retirement savings, it is essential to have separate savings to cover short-term expenses in an emergency and some education costs. Since everyone faces these financial demands at some point, having "rainy-day" savings is the only way to continue saving for retirement while taking care of immediate needs.

Since it takes time to turn saved money into wealth, *the effect of saving in the early years of adulthood is far greater than anything saved later*. In fact, for those with modest incomes, buying a dream car or house or other luxury products in one's 20s or early-30s is likely to create debt and have disastrous consequences later in life. Money spent on luxuries or the interest associated with paying for them could be in investment accounts instead, growing in value and *earning* interest and dividends over many years. So, while young people may not want to hear it, if they are disciplined early in life there will be plenty of time later to have a more expensive and impressive lifestyle.

DIVERSIFIED ASSETS: INVESTMENTS, REAL PROPERTY, AND ASSET ALLOCATION

Those who save should not keep "all their eggs in one basket." Instead, they should *diversify their investments*. This principle applies to buying, holding, or selling bank account deposits (cash), certificates of deposit (CDs, or long-term cash), stocks, bonds, and mutual funds. But the concept of diversification also applies to a broader perspective of seeing all these financial instruments as one kind of asset to be balanced by others, such as real estate or collectibles.

Unfortunately, many Americans ignored the need for diversification during the recent housing boom. Instead, they did so little saving that 75% of the wealth held by the average American family in 2010 came from the net worth of their home (the value of the home minus outstanding mortgage and other house-related debts). And that average included a large number of people who borrowed from the equity in their homes in order to spend more than their entire income to have a better lifestyle. This tactic led to a spike in the number of second mortgages and home equity loans, a sign people thought of their home as a giant piggy bank that could provide extra income in the short term and wealth later. So, while 75% of American wealth was in homes, many families had no savings or home equity at all. Apparently, many Americans had come to believe owning a home, even one heavily mortgaged, would make this all come out alright in the end.

The dangers of thinking of a house as your main source of wealth have become painfully obvious in recent years. According to the U.S. Department of Housing and Urban Development (HUD), home values declined 30.9% from 2006 to 2011. But they dropped 50% in some markets. As a result, by 2012, 25% of homeowners owed more on their mortgages than their homes were worth, a condition banks call being "*underwater*" or "*upside down.*" There were also 7 million American homeowners in or facing *foreclosure* (the bank seizing their home) because they no longer could make mortgage payments or didn't see why they should keep paying for an asset worth less than it would cost them by the time the mortgage was paid off. While the housing crisis eased in 2013, many who faced foreclosure or being upside down are still having difficulty generating wealth. After all, in foreclosure, you lose all the equity built up in your home, and the home itself. When you are upside down, you may keep your house, but it has negative equity. So it diminishes your net wealth. And these circumstances have lingered for many people.

Beyond this immediate housing crisis, even when house values are stable or going up, it is foolish to count on a home to create wealthy. This is true for two reasons.

THE COST OF OWNERSHIP

Most people spend some of their saved money as a *down payment* when they buy a house. Then, to pay for the rest of the house, they get a *mortgage,* which is paid off with interest and fees, usually over the next 30 years. And lastly, they spend money while living in their house on maintenance, home improvements, and taxes. For those who live in a home for 20 years or more there are also "extra" expenses like replacing a roof or driveway; upgrading windows, insulation, and siding; and perhaps updating bathrooms and a kitchen. Each of these projects may cost thousands or tens of thousands of dollars and must be included in the long-term cost of homeownership.

We will discuss mortgages in a later chapter. For now it is worth noting that in most markets the inflation-adjusted value of a home when it is sold rarely surpasses the total amount spent on it. However, this does not mean buying a house is a bad idea. Owning a home comes with tax benefits, and its overall costs must be compared to the cost of renting. An accountant can help you weigh the financial benefits and costs of renting versus owning. Perhaps more important, homeownership gives you something valuable beyond any financial calculation. It gives you a place to raise a family, educate children, and enjoy long-term relationships with neighbors. While it is impossible to put a financial value on these benefits, they are the best reasons to own a home.

CASHING YOUR CHIPS

When you sell your house, you will likely spend the profit you make, *if* there is any, on your next place to live. After all, if your house has gained in value, other places you might want to live probably have gone up in price as well. The only exceptions to this rule are when you sell the last house you will ever own or move from an expensive housing market to a less expensive one. The latter exception, of course, assumes you will never want or need to move back to an expensive housing market. If that happens, all you have done is put off spending the profit you made when you bought into the less expensive real estate market.

✦

None of this logic about the value of the house in which you live (your "*primary residence*") should be confused with owning *investment properties*. Some people have done very well creating wealth by owning doctors' offices, office or apartment buildings, second homes that are rented to others, or retail properties. But this strategy requires an ability and willingness to manage properties, keep them occupied, maintain the properties physically, deal with tenants, and perhaps manage a person hired to do these jobs for you. It is also important to buy and sell investment properties at the right time in the price cycle of that market. Put simply, the wealth-generating strategy of owning investment properties is not for people who think properties will always go up in value, manage themselves, or automatically generate enough income to pay all costs along the way.

INVESTING IN OTHERS' ECONOMIC ACTIVITY

If it is unwise to only invest in property and most people are unable or uninterested in owning their own business, where else can you invest savings? Luckily, governments at the local, state, and federal levels and corporations need *your* money to do *their* business, either by borrowing your money (usually as bonds) or by selling you a piece of their enterprise (usually as shares of company stock). Most money saved for retirement is invested in these kinds of assets in the hope of getting a return on that money in the form of interest, dividends, or growth of the value of the shares or mutual fund units owned.

This book is not an investment primer. There are stockbrokers, financial planners, and bank and insurance company investment counselors who can help you with these decisions. However, when evaluating their advice, remember that the best strategy is to diversify your holdings across several sectors of the economy (energy, raw materials, manufacturing, financial companies, retail/service businesses, small and large companies, etc.), a variety of financial products (stocks, corporate and government bonds, etc.), and even some foreign companies and governments.

Just as important, *re-invest the dividends and interest you earn.* Remember, this income belongs to your future, not your present lifestyle. Also, avoid the urge to stop saving in bad economic times because you think it best to keep money on the sidelines until the economy turns around. While it is often said the trick to investing is to "buy low and sell high," it is impossible for the average investor to predict or recognize when the market or a particular mutual fund or stock is at a low (about to go up in value) or at a high (about to drop in value). Neither can stockbrokers or financial planners with any consistency. If they could "time" the market that accurately, they would not need to earn a living by giving you investment advice. Rather, invest a little at a time in good times and bad times, a strategy investment advisors call *"dollar cost averaging."* With this strategy, the *average* cost of the assets you buy will allow you to grow your money. And you will avoid the risk of mistiming your decisions of when to buy or sell.

That being said, don't be afraid to take a stockbroker's or financial advisor's advice about what to buy or sell. But research the investments suggested, ask about fees that will diminish your returns, and check periodically to see how well you are doing against similar stocks and mutual funds. Also be careful if an advisor recommends constantly changing your holdings. This is often a way to generate excessive fees for the advisor, which diminishes the growth of your investments. So, while it is a bad idea to jump from one broker to another on a regular basis, don't be afraid to change advisors if your investments are not doing well over a *long* period or you are uncomfortable with your advisor's advice or way of communicating with you. After all, your investments belong to you and there is nothing to be gained by being intimidated by someone else or their opinions.

Lastly, once your money is invested, resist the urge to quickly sell investments that are going down. But don't be afraid to change investments if you feel there is a better *long-term strategy* for you or if your investment goals change. And even in the worst of times, *don't panic* or think it would be better to focus on a single investment strategy like selling everything to buy gold or only investing in high-tech companies or bonds. No matter what the current situation, remember that, especially for those with modest incomes, holding diversified investments helps weather a storm in one kind of asset, one part of the economy, or even one part of the world, while other assets hold their value or increase. History teaches us this will always be the best strategy for creating wealth.

CHAPTER 4

GROWING YOUR WEALTH: THE POWERS OF INFLATION AND COMPOUND INTEREST

Questions: How do I safely grow my money fast enough? How will inflation affect the value of the money I save? What is the difference between simple and compound interest?

INFLATION

One of the most difficult factors to predict in calculating future income needs is *inflation*. Inflation is the tendency over time for things to cost more.

Inflation varies from year to year. Recently, we have had many years of moderate inflation, a few of high inflation (*hyperinflation*), and one in which the cost of living dropped (*deflation*). Despite this variability, people who are beginning to save have to make an educated guess about what inflation will do over the next 30 to 40 years, the period before retirement. This estimate is equally important for newly-retired people, since they may live for more than 20 years *after* retirement. In fact, a recent analysis by the Employee Benefit Research Council predicted *the average American who retires today will live for another 16 ½ years.*

Given the uncertainty associated with future inflation, it helps to turn to recent history as a guide. According to the U.S. Department of the Treasury, inflation has averaged 2.65% per year in the United States since 2000, and 3.0% over the last twenty-five years. However, from 1976-1987, the annual inflation rate was 7.0%, with an amazingly high three-year average of 12.0% from 1979 to 1981. By contrast, the 2010 inflation rate was -1.8%, a key indicator of our having been in a recent significant recession.

Each person has to decide what to do with these numbers. To me, 25 years is long enough to give a good sense of what will happen in the near future. So, a *3% inflation rate* is a reasonable estimate to use in our calculations. While inflation might turn out to be higher, it might also be lower. For example, because of the hyperinflation of 1976 to 1981, a 1996 Met Life Insurance Company retirement planning booklet my parents used in their retirement years predicted an inflation rate of 5% per year over the next 20 years. But the actual rate, 2.65%, turned out to be much lower. When it comes to the reasonableness of a prediction of 3.0%, it is worth noting that the Social Security Administration projects a 2.8% annual inflation rate for the next 22 years, the longest period for which it does estimates.

Chart 4-1 illustrates the effects of a 3% inflation rate on $1,000. But first we need a little explanation. In the first year, inflation is applied to that $1,000. So in year-2, it will take $1,030 to buy what $1,000 bought a year earlier. In the following year, 3% is applied to $1,030, not just the original $1,000. So in year-3 it will take $1,061 to buy the same goods or services. By year-4, it will take $1,093. And this pattern continues in future years. *With each year, inflation stays the same in percentage terms, but its effect grows in dollar amount,* a mechanism we will soon see also applies to compound interest. Now let's turn to Chart 3-1 to see how inflation of 3% per year over 40 years would affect how much money it will take to equal the buying power of $1,000 today.

CHART 4-1: INFLATION AT 3% ON $1,000

End of Year	Amount it will take to equal $1,000 in today's dollars
1	1,030
2	1,061
3	1,093
4	1,126
5	1,159
6	1,194
7	1,230
8	1,267
9	1,305
10	1,344
11	1,384
12	1,426
13	1,469
14	1,513
	...at this point, your money has lost about 1/3 of its value
15	1,558
16	1,605
17	1,653
18	1,702
19	1,754
20	1,806
21	1,860
22	1,916
23	1,974
24	2,033
	...at this point, your money has lost about ½ of its value
25	2,094
26	2,158
27	2,222
28	2,289

End of Year	Amount it will take to equal $1,000 in today's dollars
29	2,358
30	2,428
31	2,501
32	2,576
33	2,654
34	2,733
35	2,815
36	2,900
37	2,987
	...at this point, your money has lost about 2/3 of its value
38	3,056
39	3,148
40	3,242

What does Chart 4-1 tell us? Saved money will be worth a lot less when it is used 30 to 40 years from now. This fact leads to two essential requirements of retirement planning:

- *Invest your money in a way that will grow it faster than inflation is eroding its value.*
- *Save enough money to have a significantly higher income in raw dollar amounts later in life than you need now.*

These two points are why it is a bad idea to keep all saved money in insured bank accounts or low-interest-yielding government bonds. If you do, your money will be safe. But in the last few years, the return on these investments has been barely more than 0%. When taken with the effect of inflation over this time, this means people who invested in "safe" financial products *lost* money. During my adulthood, with the exception of the period of hyperinflation in the late 1970s, this has always been the case. In other words, *avoiding all risk is the riskiest investment strategy of all*. Remember, the goal is to average more than the inflation rate for a very long time.

✦

At retirement, Chart 4-1 should be used in a different way. The income available in year-1 of retirement will continue to lose value over the following years. By year-24 of retirement, for those lucky enough to live that long, a "fixed income" will only buy half what it bought in year-1 of retirement. So, to maintain the same lifestyle, people need enough wealth at retirement to leave some of its returns unused. Or they could continue to contribute to savings. These strategies would allow savings to generate more income later.

Inflation also has an important effect on the cost of loans that are paid back over a long time. For example, if inflation averages 3% per year, the last payment on a 30-year mortgage is made with dollars that will only buy 42% of what the first payment bought. So, the last payment is much less than the first one, at least in terms of what else could be bought with that money. Thus, inflation makes the cost of a mortgage less than it appears when you buy a house and look ahead to 360 seemingly equal payments over the next 30 years.

COMPOUND RETURNS: INTEREST, DIVIDENDS, AND GROWTH

Given the importance of growing money while inflation is shrinking it, Chart 4-2 illustrates several scenarios in which a person earns *compound returns* of *more* than 3% per year by leaving both the original saved money and its yearly returns (interest, dividends, and growth) in an investment account for 40 years. As with inflation, we will start with $1,000 in today's dollars.

CHART 4-2: COMPOUND INTEREST AND THE GROWTH OF MONEY

Growth of $1,000: (rounded to nearest dollar)

End of Year	at 5%	at 6%	at 7%	at 8%
1	1,050	1,060	1,070	1,080
2	1,103	1,124	1,145	1,166
3	1,158	1,191	1,224	1,260
4	1,216	1,263	1,310	1,361
5	1,276	1,338	1,403	1,469
6	1,340	1,419	1,500	1,587
7	1,407	1,504	1,605	1,714
8	1,478	1,594	1,717	1,851
9	1,551	1,690	1,837	1,999*
10	1,629	1,791	1,966*	2,159
11	1,711	1,898	2,103	2,332
12	1,796	2,012*	2,251	2,518
13	1,886	2,133	2,408	2,719
14	1,980*	2,261	2,577	2,937
15	2,079	2,397	2,757	3,172*
16	2,183	2,541	2,950*	3,426
17	2,292	2,693	3,157	3,700
18	2,407	2,855	3,378	3,996*
19	2,527	3,026*	3,614	4,316
20	2,654	3,207	3,867	4,661
21	2,786	3,400	4,138*	5,034*
22	2,926	3,604	4,427	5,436
23	3,072*	3,820	4,737	5,871
24	3,226	4,049*	5,069*	6,341*
25	3,387	4,292	5,424	6,848
26	3.556	4,550	5,803	7,396*
27	3,734	4,823	6,209*	7,988*
28	3,921	5,112*	6,644	8,627
29	4,117*	5,419	7,139*	9,337*
30	4,322	5,744	7,607	10,084*
31	4,539	6,088*	8,139*	10,890*

End of Year	at 5%	at 6%	at 7%	at 8%
32	4,765	6,454	8,709	11,762*
33	5,004*	6,840	9,318*	12,702*
34	5,254	7,251*	9,971*	13,719*
35	5,517	7,686	10,669	14,816*
36	5,792	8,148*	11,415*	16,001*
37	6,082*	8,636	12,214*	17,282*
38	6,386	9,155*	13,069*	18,664*
39	6,705	9,704	13,984*	20,157*
40	7,041*	10,286*	14,963*	21,770*

Note: *Starred numbers* represent saved money increasing by roughly $1,000 or more, the amount contributed to savings in year 1.

Chart 4-2 illustrates four important points.

- Compound interest makes money grow faster than most people guess. And *the pace of growth accelerates as time goes on*. For example, at a 7% rate of return, $1,000 doubles in 10½ years, adds an extra $1,000 in the next 6 years, then again in about 4½ years, 3½ years, 2½ years, 2¼ years, and so on until it adds an extra $1,000 in just over one year. In short, *the "older" your money, the faster it grows*.

- There is a huge difference between saving for 30 versus 40 years. At 7%, 52% of the growth of money put away in the first year comes from the last 10 years of a 40-year saving plan. This is just another way of saying older money grows faster.

- *There is a great difference in getting a "little higher" return*. Many people think the difference between 5% and 7% is 2%. This is not true. The real difference is 40%, since 7 is 40% greater than 5. As a result, at 7% you end up with *more than twice* the money from your first year of saving than you would get from 5%.

- If, however, saved money earned *simple interest*, it would get the same interest every year based on the initial investment amount. So, in the 7% column, you would add $70 each year, which would generate $3,800 after 40 years. This is why *compound interest is so much more "powerful" as a wealth generator than simple interest.*

Over the last few years of my teaching career I taught 5th graders percentages by having them develop compound and simple interest charts. Students used their charts to calculate the interest they would pay for various lengths of time on borrowed money versus the interest they would earn on saved money. So I know from experience these are not difficult concepts to grasp and how powerful this knowledge can be in shaping how a person looks at debt and saving. Put simply, *understanding compound interest, inflation, time, and the interaction among the three is the key to eventually having a big enough retirement "nest egg."*

SAVING THROUGH THE YEARS

Chart 4-2 demonstrates the way compound interest grows your *first year*'s savings. But the real question for someone trying to create wealth is "what will happen if I save each year for 30 to 40 years and invest all that money and its returns along the way?"

A brief explanation is needed here. In Chart 3-2, the $1,000 saved in the first year will have 40 years to grow. In the 7% column, that $1,000 will become $14,963. But $1,000 saved in the second year will "only" have 39 years to grow. So it will become $13,984, while $1,000 saved in the third year will grow for 38 years and become $13,069. This pattern will continue in the following years.

So the $1,000 saved a year before retirement will only grow to $1,070. Notice that these are the numbers in the 7% column in reverse order.

We are now ready to use Chart 4-2 to see how much money you would have after 40 years of saving and investing $1,000 each year. All we have to do is add all the numbers in one column. Let's do this for each rate of return, remembering that *in all four cases you contribute $1,000 per year, for a total of $40,000.* Here are the results *before we take inflation and taxes into account.* For a 5% return, you end up with $126,855. For a 6% return, you end up with $164,045. For 7%, you end up with $213,450. And lastly, for 8% you end up with $290,145.

These are wonderful results. But are they realistic? Yes. It is possible to average a 7% to 8% return over a long period on money that is shielded from taxes and invested with a risk profile meant to create growth. For example, the New York State Teachers' Retirement Fund has averaged 8.8% returns over the last 20 years and is predicting annual returns of 8.0% for the next decade. However, it is important to note that nobody's returns are the same every year. There may be years when returns are more than a 10%, years when they are less than 5%, and bleak years when savings lose value. Moreover, with a shorter period before your saved money will have to be used, as retirement approaches it becomes more important to protect against a bad year. So some, but not all, saved money should be moved to lower-risk investments that are likely to generate lower rates of return. Thus, as a person ages, his or her return might move from the 8% or 7% column to the 6% or 5% column. That is why we will use a pre-retirement return of 7% in many examples in later chapters.

At any point in this process, if *you* know you have enough savings for retirement, lower your risk to preserve your savings while retaining some potential for moderate growth. In that case, you might receive an average of 5% return on your money for a substantial period before retirement. This is what many people do after retirement.

The goal is to achieve a balance. *Take only as much risk as you can tolerate and need to take.* When you no longer need to grow your money as fast, rebalance your investments to take less risk. Lastly, do not trust anyone who guarantees consistent returns of 10% or higher. Trying to get these returns *legally* over many years involves a level of risk that should be avoided. Remember the old saying, "If it seems too good to be true, it probably is." In short, while fear should not keep you from taking some risk as an investor, it is equally important to avoid being swindled out of your money by your own greed as you ignore risk altogether.

THE SAVINGS BOTTOM LINE: GROWTH, INFLATION, AND TAXES

To figure out how much saved money will be *worth* after putting aside $1,000 every year for 30 to 40 years, we must know how much inflation will diminish the value of money by the time of retirement. We can arrive at this calculation by using Chart 4-1 in the same way we used Chart 4-2. If you save $1,000 each year for 40 years, by the time you retire the money saved in the first year will have been eroded by inflation for 40 years. The money saved in the second year will have eroded for 39 years, and so on until the money saved one year before retirement will only lose 3% of its value. In other words, *the earliest dollars saved have the longest period in which to grow because of compound interest and the longest period to lose value because of inflation.*

By combining the effects of inflation on the money saved each year, we can arrive at an *average* for the deflation of all the money saved. After 30 years, saved money will erode *on average* to 60% (3/5) of the value it had when the saver chose not to spend it and saved it instead. After 40 years, it will erode to an average of 51.5%.

We are getting closer to assessing the result of saving. But there is one variable we have not taken into account: *the contribution the government makes to retirement savings through its tax policies.* While it is impossible to know for sure what will happen to tax laws in the future, at present most modest-income households are in the 15% or 25% federal income tax brackets. So, the *last* dollars earned are taxed at a 15% or 25% rate. However, if a dollar is put into a tax-deferred retirement account, it is not taxed in that year. So, taxable income drops by one dollar and the tax owed drops by 15 or 25 cents. Thus, the federal government reduces taxes of a household in the 25% bracket that contributes $1,000 by $250, which makes the "out-of-pocket" contribution only $750. Similarly, a household in the 15% bracket must spend $850 "out of pocket" to save $1,000.

Now let's look at the bottom line for a return of 7%, using a 15% tax bracket and 3% inflation rate. A taxpayer who saves $1,000 a year for 30 years contributes $25,500 while the federal government provides $4,500 through tax savings. This will generate an inflation-adjusted $63,125. Meanwhile, a taxpayer who saves for 40 years contributes $34,000 while the government contributes $6,000. This will generate an inflation-adjusted $109,930.

The bad news is savers will not be as wealthy as they thought they would become. The good news is they will stay well ahead of inflation and become wealthier than they would have been if they hadn't saved. In any case, modest-income households with reasonable savings plans save much more than $1,000 per year. So a consistent saver will achieve totals much higher than the above figures. Most important, whatever the eventual total, that money will be available in retirement to generate a significant part of the income needed to sustain a good lifestyle. In other words, savers will be much better off later in life because of their savings habits while they were income earners.

CHAPTER 5

DEBT PART 1: MORTGAGES

Questions: What kind of mortgage should I get? How does mortgage interest work? Why do I end up having to pay back so much?

Few of us go through life without borrowing money. There are times when borrowing is necessary and sensible, as for a home, education, car, or other large ticket item. But there are times when Americans borrow for less necessary items, borrow more than they can handle, or accept terms of repayment that make debt harder to handle than it needs to be.

There is no more complex financial subject than debt. To keep things manageable, we will focus on the loans most families use to make purchases, either because they do not have enough money when they buy or because they want to "smooth out" the pain of buying goods or services by paying for them *after* making the purchase. We will assume for the purposes of this discussion you are up to date on your taxes. But if you owe back taxes, this is the first debt you should settle, since the IRS or your state tax authority may seize other assets and some of your pay to recover what you owe them. This alone would make saving for retirement and emergencies impossible.

There are seven common categories of consumer debt:

- *Mortgages* allow many Americans to buy a home.
- *Credit cards* issued by financial institutions allow people to make purchases, get cash advances, or cover bank overdrafts.
- *Student loans* offered by institutions of higher learning, the federal government, states, and banks allow a student or his or her family to put off paying for part of higher education until after graduation or leaving school.
- *Retail credit cards,* most commonly issued by "big box" and department stores, let consumers purchase items "on time."
- *Auto loans* offered by car companies extend credit to customers who are purchasing vehicles. Financial institutions also provide auto loans.
- *Home equity loans and second mortgages* offered by financial institutions allow homeowners to use the part of their house they have paid for (their home equity) to pay for home repairs or other expenses. The homeowner receives cash up front and "recaptures" the equity when he or she pays off the loan or second mortgage.
- *Personal loans* from friends and family are used to pay for essential or discretionary costs with no, little, or unique interest arrangements.

Each kind of debt carries different conditions. But with the exception of some personal loans, the borrower has to pay back the money borrowed (the *principal*), *interest,* and perhaps *fees*, the latter two of which are the cost of using (renting) someone else's money for a time. Since interest associated with borrowing can become a large budget expense, understanding how it is calculated and what it will cost is an important part of any family's financial planning.

In this chapter, we will look at mortgages, leaving other kinds of debt to Chapter 6.

MORTGAGES: HOME SWEET HOME

Most people never save enough to buy a home. So, most homebuyers "take out" or "get" a mortgage. This is the largest loan most families ever have.

Years ago, homebuyers were required to make a *down payment* of 20% of the price of the home they were buying. But as house prices rose and government agencies and banks changed their policies to encourage homeownership, down payments shrank. Finally, at the height of the housing boom from 1990 to 2007, many homebuyers were able to get a mortgage (and a home) with no down payment at all.

The good news is this made it easier to buy a house. The bad news is people who lacked the income or assets needed for homeownership got mortgages, while those who would have always qualified for a mortgage were able to buy more expensive homes than they would have in earlier times. The easy availability of mortgage money also drove up home prices in desirable housing markets, leaving many homebuyers with overly large monthly payments. But the way financial institutions packaged and promoted mortgages made the problem even worse.

FIXED-RATE MORTGAGES

When a person applies for a mortgage, a bank, credit union, or mortgage-company decides *if* he or she is qualified to borrow, how much can be borrowed, fees payable as part of the mortgage, and the mortgage interest rate. Factors influencing these decisions include the Prime Interest Rate ("*the Prime*"), the interest rate charged to banks and governments when they borrow money from the Federal Reserve Bank ("*the Fed*") to do their daily business; the value of the home bought; the bank's opinion about future inflation and house prices; and the applicant's *(mortgagee's)* household income, credit worthiness, and net worth (assets minus debts).

There is nothing you can do about the assessed value of the home you hope to buy except buy a less expensive house. Nor can you influence the Prime or a bank's opinion about future economic prospects or house values.

Let's take a brief look at the Prime. When the Fed wants to slow down the economy to fight inflation it raises the Prime. This increases the interest rates banks charge to their customers. This, in turn, discourages companies and individuals from borrowing, which decreases their spending and the economic activity generated by that spending. When the Fed wants to stimulate the economy, as in a recession, it lowers the Prime to make "cheap credit" available to individuals and businesses. This encourages spending in all sectors of our economy.

Changes in the Prime directly affect the rate of return on savings accounts, bonds, and certificates of deposit, as well as the interest rates charged on all loans in the United States. That is why mortgage rates offered by different financial institutions are usually similar. Nevertheless, it is important to *shop around for the best mortgage deal*. Sometimes, a financial institution will have a slightly lower interest rate than others or offer lower *points and closing costs* (fees). As "preferred customers," homebuyers might get a better rate from the bank where they have savings and checking accounts. Or, they might get a better deal from a credit union devoted to their local area or their employment or social group. Or lastly, they might get a better rate from an online mortgage website. Given the size of mortgages, this is one area of spending where it pays to do extensive comparative shopping.

The mortgage rate *you* get depends on your household income, assets, debts, and credit scores. Your *credit scores* (there are three main rating agencies) are one factor you can influence. So find out what they are. They will be low (bad) if you have been behind on loan payments, have a lot of other debts, have defaulted on other loans, or have recently taken on new loans or credit cards. If you have low scores, try to improve them before applying for a mortgage. If not, you will be given a higher interest rate. After all, *low scores mean you are less likely to pay back the loan*. So mortgage lenders will want a higher return on *their* money to justify taking that higher risk.

There is no guarantee you will get the wonderful interest rate you see on television. The only way to find out is to apply. The rate that will determine how much you will have to pay back is called *the APR* ("actual percentage rate"). The APR is calculated by adding up all fees *and* interest payable over the life of the mortgage, and then representing the *annual* cost of these charges as a percentage of the principal. Since fees may vary greatly from one mortgage provider to another, *the APR is the only number you should use to compare loan offers*.

Traditional mortgage payment schedules are based on an *amortization chart*, which calculates how interest is applied to the principal borrowed. To cite an imaginary example, if a home sells for $220,000 and the homebuyer makes a down-payment of $22,000 (10%), the mortgage principal is $198,000. With an APR of 5%, $9,900 (5% x $198,000) is added as interest and fees in the first year of re-payment. So, if mortgage payments total $12,000 a year, in the first year $9,900 goes to interest and fees and $2,100 to paying off principal. In the second year, 5% is charged on the remaining principal, which is now $195,900. Hence, that year's $12,000 payments cover $9,795 of interest and fees and $2,205 of principal. In other words, amortization works in reverse to compound interest. The interest rate stays the same, which is why this is called a *fixed-rate mortgage*. But interest is applied to a smaller and smaller amount each year.

To calculate the monthly payment, the lender adds up the original principal, interest, and fees payable over the life of the mortgage, which gives the lender the total payback amount. Then all *monthly payments* are made equal. Since mortgage payments have to fit into your budget, *this is the number that tells you how much you can pay for a house*. Traditionally people were advised to limit house costs (mortgage payments, school and property taxes, home insurance, etc.) to no more than 25% of net annual income. But many current sources recommend a more liberal 30% to 35%. An accountant or financial planner can help you decide how much house *you* can afford.

Mortgage lenders may add property tax and home insurance premiums to mortgage payments to protect themselves against the possibility of the mortgagee failing to pay these bills while the lender owns part of the house. But this is not an extra cost. Whether they are part of a mortgage payment or bills paid separately, the homeowner would still have to pay these amounts.

Closing costs and points, which cover the bank's cost of initiating a mortgage, must be paid up-front. But they are *not* part of the down payment because they do not reduce the principal owed. Since they may add up to thousands of dollars, it is important to question and understand these charges before signing a mortgage. If a homebuyer has enough savings, he or she may also make a larger down payment than the lender demands, which would lower the principal and total interest cost. But if you get a good mortgage interest rate, it might *not* make sense to take money from investment accounts that are earning higher rates of return. Lastly, it is important to *have a lawyer or escrow officer examine mortgage documents, deed, and title papers* associated with the house you are buying before signing a mortgage or the purchase agreement for your home.

COMPARING MORTGAGES AND REPAYMENT STRATEGIES

Let's look at two real-life examples of 30-year fixed rate mortgages that came from Quicken Loans' online amortization chart in September 2011.

The total payback for a $200,000 fixed-rate mortgage with a 6% APR was $431,677, with $231,677 going to interest, title insurance, and fees. *In the first 15 years, the principal shrinks to $150,000*. So, if the house is sold after 15 years, the homebuyer still owes $150,000. This is crucial. Many homeowners incorrectly assume they would owe $100,000. After all, they are halfway through the mortgage term and have made half the payments. But, three quarters of their payments have gone to pay interest and fees. However, if a homeowner makes one extra payment a year, in a strategy called "*mortgage acceleration*," the principal shrinks to $125,000 in 15 years. So, 15 extra payments of $1,000 ($15,000) turn into a $25,000 benefit. If the house is not sold, the mortgage would be paid off in 26 years instead of 30, with a payback of $400,095, saving $31,572.

For a similar mortgage with a *5% APR*, the total payback was $386,513. But if the homeowner accelerates the mortgage, it is paid off in 26 years with a payback of $358,378, saving $30,135. With a 30-year term, the outstanding principal after 15 years is $140,000, while accelerated payments reduce the principal to $118,000 in 15 years.

These examples demonstrate the difference between a 5% and a 6% APR. As with interest earned on savings, the difference between 5% and 6% is not 1%. It is 20%, the difference between 5 and 6. As a result, if a homeowner pays off a mortgage in 30 years, a 5% APR mortgage costs $49,164 less than a 6% APR mortgage. If paid off in 26 years, the saving is $39,717. Chart 5-1 illustrates the savings associated with getting a lower APR and/or accelerating mortgage payments.

CHART 5-1: COMPARISON OF TWO 30-YEAR FIXED RATE $200,000 MORTGAGES

APR	Monthly Payment	Total Payback, including Fees	Years to pay off Mortgage		Principal after 15 years of payments	
			No accel.	With accel.	No accel.	With accel.
6%	$1,199	$432,677	30	26	$150,000	$125,000
5%	$1,074	$386,513	30	26	$140,000	$120,000

Before leaving this topic, let's pause to take a closer look at the mortgage acceleration strategy. While mortgage APRs have historically averaged about 8%, they presently range from 3.5% to 6%. And in most cases the interest paid on mortgages is tax deductible. So, people with mortgages save on their income taxes, a fact that makes the mortgage interest rate paid out of their own pockets (the "*effective interest rate*") lower than 3.5% to 6%.

In this tax and interest environment, it makes more sense to put "extra" money that might go toward a thirteenth mortgage payment into retirement accounts. After all, while it is shocking to realize it will cost over $400,000 to pay for a $200,000 house, invested money may double in as little as 10 years. In other words, saved money usually grows by more than a mortgage's effective interest rate. However, if we return to higher interest rates or mortgage interest is no longer tax deductible in the future (already the case in Canada), the balance may shift to paying off a mortgage as quickly as possible. So, talk to an accountant about which choice is best for you. Just remember, if you fail to put money that would have gone to a thirteenth mortgage payment into savings, you will be worse off than if you had made the extra mortgage payment.

No matter how they handle their mortgage, most people are shocked that at least 50% of their payments go to interest and fees. It is important to remember, however, that as a result of inflation mortgage payments are made with increasingly deflated dollars. So, the payments made over the life of a 2012 mortgage are not really as much as they seem, at least in 2012 dollars.

REFINANCING: TRADING OLD DEBT FOR NEW DEBT

As interest rates reached historic lows in the last few years, people with mortgages looked for ways to replace them with new mortgages. In response, financial institutions offered *refinancing ("re-fi")* plans, in which a homeowner gets a new mortgage with a lower interest rate and uses its principal to pay off the old mortgage. Currently, financial institutions are offering 10 to 30 year re-fi plans with APRs as low as 3.25%. This leaves the borrower with lower monthly payments for the new term, which can usually be matched to the remaining part of the old term.

This makes a lot of sense. Why pay 7% interest on a mortgage for its remaining years if you can pay 4%? In fact, for mortgages with 10 or more years to go, even a half percentage point drop in APR can make a big difference. However, most refinancing deals come with new up-front fees and other charges that may add up to several thousand dollars. More important, these deals are usually only available to homeowners who have at least 20% equity in their home relative to its *current* value or who can make a new down payment of up to 20% when they refinance.

Herein lays the catch for many homeowners. If they bought a house for $200,000 and the house has lost 25% of its value, it is now worth $150,000. So, if they still owe $150,000 of principal on their mortgage, they have no equity at all. To get refinancing, they must make a down payment of $30,000 (20% x $150,000) and pay new fees and closing costs. Meanwhile, many homeowners are completely disqualified from refinancing if the value of their home has dropped by *more* than 25% since the old mortgage was written, a circumstance that is unfortunately common in many housing markets.

Homeowners who have equity in their homes and good credit are sometimes offered great re-fi deals with *no* closing costs. But other homeowners don't qualify at all or must pay up-front costs they cannot afford. So, refinancing often fails to reach those who need it most. In response, in 2009 the federal government created the *Home Affordable Refinance Program* (*HARP*) to help distressed mortgage owners get refinancing. Nevertheless, to date, many distressed homeowners are still unable to get refinancing.

VARIABLE RATE, SUB-PRIME AND BALLOON PAYMENT MORTGAGES

Given the high monthly payments associated with mortgages and the desire to ensure profits for themselves and the maximum number of buyers, over the last 20 years financial institutions have created several non-traditional mortgages.

In a *variable mortgage*, the interest rate is based on the *current* Prime. Meanwhile, fixed-rate mortgages are based on long-term projections of the Prime, a calculation that nowadays always gives a higher interest rate than the rate for variable mortgages. This makes a variable mortgage look like a great deal. But there is a catch. *If the Prime goes up, so does the APR*. Given today's low Prime, this is virtually certain to happen. As a result, there is no way to know how much future mortgage payments will be. This makes it impossible to budget for housing costs, leaving a homebuyer at risk at some point of not having enough income to live in the home.

As bad as variable mortgages are, there are versions of it that are even worse. During the housing boom, banks offered some homebuyers variable mortgages at *below* the Prime Rate. This can only be called a "bait and switch" product. After all, banks were lending money at a lower rate than they were paying to borrow money from the Fed to operate their own business. Like a drug dealer giving a customer the first "hit" at a reduced price, the only way a bank could make a profit on *sub-prime mortgages*, as these loans are called, was to raise the interest rate as soon as possible. By then the homeowner was "hooked" and had to pay the higher payments.

Lastly, some banks offered *balloon payment mortgages*. In these mortgages, which are more commonly used for commercial properties, the borrower pays a low monthly payment that covers interest and little or no principal. If no principal is paid, the loan is called an *interest-only mortgage*. In both cases, the borrower must pay a huge "balloon" payment at the end of the mortgage that will cover the remaining principal and interest.

✦

Why would anyone agree to one of these non-traditional mortgages? First, some homebuyers didn't understand what they were signing, trusting their bank's recommendation. Second, some buyers only cared that their initial payments were low without thinking about the long-term consequences. Third, many buyers wanted to buy more home in order to have a fancier lifestyle. And finally, many assumed home prices would keep going up, as they had in most places over the previous 20 years. If mortgage payments became too high, they would sell the house and make a profit, even after paying off the remaining principal. With balloon payment mortgages, the price of a property would have to go up so much that it could be sold or refinanced at the end of the term to cover the balloon payment, with the homeowner keeping the difference.

To say these strategies have not worked is a gross understatement. Many homeowners have had their mortgage payments increased to more than twice the initial "teaser rate." Meanwhile, house prices have declined, in some places by 50%. The result has been a double whammy: mortgage payments that are too high to pay, and house prices that are too low to sell and end up with enough money to pay off the remaining principal. For those in this hole, the options are limited. Foreclosure, abandoning a home, or selling it for less than the existing principal with their bank's approval (a deal called a *short sale*) offer little to a homeowner's short-term economic well-being.

In passing, it is worth noting that many homebuyers are drawn to the idea of buying a short-sale or foreclosed house because of its low price in relation to its previous (and hopefully future) value. However, this strategy may involve unforeseen difficulties. The seller of a short-sale house is not free to sell without bank approval, and that approval may be delayed or withdrawn, despite assurances from real estate agents or the bank holding the mortgage. Moreover, short-sale houses are sold "as is," while foreclosed houses, which may also be tied up in bank "red tape," are often abandoned, vandalized, or stripped of appliances and other items by the time the deal is done. In both cases, this leaves the new owner responsible for major repairs. Thus, while this sometimes turns out to be a way to get a great deal on a home, the old adage remains true: "buyer beware."

✦

Despite the above risks, *you* can avoid the main house-buying pitfalls by following seven rules.

- *Get your credit scores in order.*

- *Only buy as much home as you can realistically afford.*

- *Make as large a down payment as you can.*

- *Only accept a fixed rate mortgage*, being sure you can budget for its payments.

- *Hire a lawyer or escrow officer* to look at all aspects of your purchase, and an *engineering inspector* to check out the house before you finalize the deal.

- *Develop a financial plan for owning a home*, paying all your other bills, and saving for the future. Without such a plan, you may end up "house poor:" owning a beautiful home but lacking the money to furnish it, pay other bills, or save for the future.

- *Accelerate your mortgage payments* if you can, if this benefits you.

No matter how responsible you are about housing and mortgage choices, of course, nothing is guaranteed in life. There may be medical emergencies, divorces, or bouts of unemployment that are impossible to foresee. But if you follow the suggestions outlined in this chapter, you stand the best chance of dodging the financial disasters that have befallen so many American homeowners. As one Rochester NY real estate agent recently put it, people could avoid many of the dangers of homeownership if they simply thought of "affordability" as an important feature of a home at the time they buy it. In fact, to me, it should be more important than walk-in closets or granite counters in the kitchen or bathrooms. In any case, if you are frugal about the choice of home you buy and sensible about the terms of your mortgage, you should be able to safely enjoy the benefits and pleasures that come with homeownership.

CHAPTER 6

DEBT PART 2, CARS, CREDIT CARDS, COLLEGE AND YOUR UNCLE CHARLIE

Questions: Why am I always in debt? Should I buy or lease my new car? How can we pay for our children's college educations without leaving us or them broke for years? How can I learn to use credit cards without running up so much debt?

IN AMERICA TODAY, YOU CAN GET A LOAN FOR JUST ABOUT ANYTHING YOU want to buy. So let's take a look at the most commonly incurred non-mortgage consumer debts.

GETTING A VEHICLE

There are three ways to get a new or used vehicle.

PAYING ALL CASH UP FRONT

You can buy a vehicle with cash for the agreed-upon price plus your state's sales tax and registration fee. People who do this are often able to negotiate the best possible price. In "the old days" many people did this, believing they should only buy a vehicle with money already saved.

CAR LOANS FOR PURCHASE

You can buy a vehicle with a loan from a bank, credit union, or the car's manufacturer. Interest is applied to the agreed-upon price plus tax and registration fee. As with a mortgage, each monthly payment includes interest and some principal, with the principal slowly diminishing and payments made equal throughout the term of the loan. You can make a down payment and borrow the balance or get a loan for the entire purchase amount. In either case, new car loans are usually written for 3 to 6 year terms. *The longer the term, the lower the monthly payments but the higher the total amount paid back.*

Car loans may seem like a bad idea because they add extra cost to your purchase. But this is one area of debt that is very complex. In bad economic conditions or at "slow" times of the year, car companies may be desperate to sell already-built cars that are costing them money as they sit on lots or at the factory. So they offer great credit deals as an incentive to prospective buyers. For example, a car company might offer a loan with no money down and 0% to 2% interest for a 3- to 5-year term. If you are shopping at the end of a model year, next year's models may be out or about to "hit the showroom floor." So, the new car you are buying is considered last year's model. This may make it possible to negotiate a reasonably low purchase price. In that case, it would be foolish to refuse the loan since the cash that would be used to buy the car can stay in investment accounts and grow over the next few years, while the loan payments incur little or no interest.

The only caution is to pay close attention to the details in the loan agreement, including extra fees; penalties for paying off the loan early; and your rights if your car needs major repairs or bodywork. Also negotiate the best price first as if you were making a cash purchase. Then ask about a loan deal. That way you can compare both deals, which will show how much the loan *really* costs. Most important, if you get a great loan, don't buy more car than you would if you were paying cash. If you take that money out of an investment account for any reason, you will not get the benefit of it growing while you pay off your wonderful car loan.

LEASING

Lastly, you can lease a vehicle, with the car company remaining the owner of the car (holding the *Title*) during the lease. In this arrangement, monthly payments add up to part of the price of the car plus interest and tax on that amount. In return, you get use of the car for 2 to 3½ years and a set number of miles (usually 10,000 to 12,000 miles per year). At the end of the lease, the car may be returned at little cost, depending on turn-in fees, excess mileage charges, and damage to the car. Or the car may be purchased for a preset amount (the *residual value*) plus tax on that amount. In that case, there is a purchase fee but no turn-in fee or charge for damages or extra mileage.

At first glance, leasing looks like the worst option. For those who turn in their car at the end of the lease, monthly payments created no equity. For those who buy the car, lease payments plus the residual value add up to more than they would have paid with any other arrangement. However, there are four reasons why leasing makes sense for some people.

First, self-employed people may be able to charge lease payments to their business, which reduces their taxable income. This changes the financial equation entirely. Second, those who take good care of their car (some luck is involved here) and drive the amount of miles in the lease agreement are able to get a new car roughly every 3 years with little hassle or extra cost. It is also rare for a leased car to require expensive out-of-warrantee repairs. So, leased cars are dependable and have low repair costs. Third, some leases come with low residual values. In fact, while it would *not* be wise to plan on this in the future, the recent recession has made used cars more expensive than anyone assumed they would be in 2009 or 2010. As a result, some leases ending in 2012 or 2013 have residual values that are well below current prices. In this situation, it makes sense to buy the car at the end of its lease. Then, if it is unwanted, sell the car yourself. Amazingly, this "flip" can be fairly profitable on some models. And fourth, given the pace at which new hybrid and electric vehicle technologies are being introduced, it might make sense to lease and wait three years to see which technologies and models fare best. Then you can make a more informed "permanent" choice for your transportation needs.

But in all cases, it is essential to know what is in your lease agreement and how it compares to your purchase options. And remember, if you damage your car or drive it many more miles than the lease allows, you will be forced to purchase it at the end of the lease or pay a lot to turn it in.

Finally, loan interest rates are higher for used cars. Hence, when considering the purchase of a used car, the higher interest rate may tip the balance toward paying cash. However, many young adults would still be better off buying a quality used car and waiting until they are financially more secure before buying or leasing a new one.

Given these variables, the decision of how to acquire a vehicle is different for different people. But in all cases limiting the vehicles you look at to those you can afford by any payment arrangement is a more important element of being "frugal" than how you pay for the vehicle you select.

EDUCATION: THE PRICE OF A SHOT AT SUCCESS

A good education helps an individual get the experience, knowledge, and credentials needed to become a more complete and successful person. For many people, education is also an enjoyable way to enrich their lives and deepen their understanding of the world around them. But none of these benefits come without a cost.

THE HIDDEN COSTS OF K-12 EDUCATION

The cost of American education is staggering. As soon as their children near school age, parents face decisions about the cost of education. If they live in a place with poor public schools, sending a child to a private school may seem necessary. American urban-suburban areas offer secular (non-religious) and parochial (run by religious organizations) private school options. However, parents must pay tuition and fees for 13 years *before* facing the cost of post-secondary education. In fact, depending on the private school selected and the availability of scholarships, a K-12 private education may cost $100,000 to $400,000 *per child*.

Faced with such steep costs, many parents explore other options. The first is to try to get a child into a well-respected "magnet" school within the local school district. The second is to enroll a child in a Charter school. While privately run, Charter schools use public school money. So they don't charge tuition. But they are not available to everyone in poorly performing school districts. Moreover, wherever Charter schools have accepted the full range of students in their communities, many have performed no better than the public schools with which they "compete." However, there may be a particularly successful or innovative Charter school in your area worth considering.

The third option is to move to a community with better schools. But this is expensive. Housing costs more, on a sliding scale that reflects the reputation of each school district. If house prices, property and school taxes, and perhaps the cost of commuting to work from a greater distance are included, the *extra* cost of owning a home in a better school district may be over $250,000 in 20 years, the time it often takes from a family's first child starting kindergarten to the last one finishing high school. If parents stay in that house as empty-nesters, the extra cost may be $375,000 or more. It is not too extreme to say this "surcharge" amounts to a tuition payment in lieu of living in a community with less successful schools and sending children to private schools. As long as we use local property-based taxes to support public education and live in economically segregated communities, the fact that *America's best public schools are quasi-tuition-based private schools in disguise* will remain a reality for all American parents.

COLLEGE AND BEYOND

However a family solves the financial issues associated with K-12 education, it is only the beginning of the price of education in the United States. If a child wants a higher education, the cost of going to a university, college, or technical school looms large over almost all family budgets.

In recognition of this problem, the federal government has authorized states to establish educational savings *529 Plans*, to which anyone can contribute starting as soon as a child is born. However, not surprisingly, most funders of 529 Plans are parents or grandparents. Each 529 Plan must name the child who will eventually use the money. And only siblings or children of the named student are allowed to use left-over money if the child does not go to college or fails to use all Plan money while in college. In other words, 529 Plans have *limited transferability*. Some 529 Plans also stipulate the money must be used within the state sponsoring the Plan. Lastly, there are 529 Plans in which a financial advisor manages the investments and ones in which the plan holder does this job. But in all cases, it is important to check the *fees* charged by the financial company managing or holding your Plan. These *can severely limit growth in a 529 Plan*.

As an alternative, some state college and university systems offer plans in which tuition is pre-paid. This has mutual benefits. The state system gets to use the money right away without paying interest, and the plan holder avoids increases in tuition later and the shock of paying for a child's education in just four years or having to pay back large student loans after school. Since the rise in college costs has consistently outstripped the return you could reasonably get on savings, this arrangement is not a bad deal. But a child has to go to one of those schools. Given the uncertainties of life over any 20 year period, it might therefore be better to save for a child's education in a 529 Plan that allows a child to go to any school in any state.

Let's take a brief look at the tax consequences of having a 529 Plan. *States with income taxes do not tax contributions to or growth within these plans*. Meanwhile, the *federal government does tax 529 Plan contributions but does not tax growth within a Plan*. The greatest saving, however, comes when the named student pays for tuition, room, board, and school supplies: *that money is not taxed as income of the holder or beneficiary of the Plan*. As a result, half of 529 Plan money spent on education may come from tax savings. In other words, the federal and state governments may pay for half of your child's education.

A 529 Plan is a good way to save for college. However, if a child does not go to a post-secondary school, the plan holder has to pay all taxes that were not paid over the years *plus* a 10% penalty to use the money for anything else. Schools also know a 529 Plan *has* to be used for education, while other parental assets may be meant for other family expenses or the parents' retirement. So, if a child applies for a scholarship, colleges weight 529 Plan savings more heavily than other assets. Hence, while it always seems unfair to parents, having *a 529 Plan may limit the scholarship assistance a child gets* from his or her college or university.

This is important because few people save enough in a 529 Plan to pay for the entire cost of a college education. Most children with 529 Plans combine that money with family assets, current parental income that can be spent on education, and scholarships. If these funds are still not enough, students may apply for loans offered by the federal and state governments, banks, and the college they attend. Children with no 529 Plan do the same, although parents may have to pay more out of savings or current income, or children may have to get larger student loans.

SCHOLARSHIPS

Most American college students pay for part of their education with scholarships. Many states offer partial scholarships to all college students who live in their state, and other scholarships based on high achievement in high school or standardized pre-college tests. Separately, the federal government offers partial scholarships (*Pell Grants*) based on financial need, while the school a child attends may offer additional scholarship help. If a student is not a star athlete offered an athletic scholarship or a star student offered an academic scholarship by the schools of his or her choice, the student may be offered a *need-based scholarship*. These are calculated by the school on the basis of the parents and in a few cases the child's income, assets, and ability to pay for a college education. Meanwhile, students from very poor families may receive "full" need-based scholarships that completely cover room, board, and tuition.

Despite these traditional practices, over the last few years several elite private universities have been giving full scholarships to a wider range of students from low- to modest-income families and partial scholarships to middle-class and wealthy students without regard to exceptional academic merit in relation to that school's admission standards. This is a good way to get top diverse and poor students as well as middle-class and wealthy students whose parents can pay the rest of the cost. Ironically, this may make the net cost of going to an elite school less than going to a less prestigious private or state school. In any case, if your child is an exceptional student these offers are worth investigating.

Unfortunately, with or without a 529 Plan, many parents are disappointed when colleges and various government agencies announce how much scholarship money their child will receive. As a result, students may consider other options for limiting the cost of college or paying for it.

WHERE TO GO

All states have *community colleges* run by municipalities and counties. These offer programs that lead to two-year associates degrees. Some of these programs prepare students for trades or technical careers, while others focus on academic subjects. The latter give weak high school graduates a second chance to become "college ready," while older students and some younger students who did well in high school attend community colleges because they are the least expensive higher education option or because they make it possible to stay close to home. Students who complete associates degrees may end their education at that point and enter the job market. Or they may transfer to a four-year college or university, where they receive credit for some or all of their community college work. In a recent expansion of their mission, community colleges are also leading the way in delivering programs for adults who need re-training to seek new jobs. Given the limited resources of most mature students, this is a great development.

All states also have *public universities and colleges* of various reputations, admission standards, and sizes. In some states, there are public colleges that specialize in one area of study, such as teacher training, engineering, art, music, or liberal arts. Meanwhile, public universities offer programs that lead to undergraduate, graduate, and professional degrees. Tuition may be higher at some public schools than others within the same state, but in-state students always get a better price than out-of-state or foreign students. Moreover, there is a similar range of *private colleges and universities,* some of which are secular while others are religious. Some focus on special areas of study. Others focus on liberal arts. And still others offer undergraduate, graduate, and professional degrees.

Lastly, there are "non-traditional" educational options. *Corporation-run for-profit schools* provide associate, undergraduate, or graduate degree programs, offering open-enrollment to all high school graduates. These schools sometimes specialize in one area of study and promise connections to jobs in related fields. However, students and parents should be careful to check out the value of these schools' credits and degrees to traditional schools and employers, especially since *for-profit schools can be even more expensive than traditional private colleges*. Given these costs and their low graduation rates in comparison to "traditional" schools, for-profit school graduates and dropouts alike are left with more debt and higher default rates on student loans than any other students. In fact, according to a recent report by the Senate Health, Education, Labor, and Pensions Committee, 10% of college students attend for-profit schools; but for-profit students account for 50% of student loan defaults. Thus, students should ensure their educational money is spent wisely, including borrowed money.

Many for-profit *and* traditional schools offer *online undergraduate and graduate degree programs*. There are even institutions that *only* offer online courses. Compared to physically going to a school and paying for room, board, and "seat time," these programs may lower the cost of post-secondary education. They also give students in isolated locations access to a wide range of programs. But the same caution applies here as with for-profit schools in general. Be sure the school is fully accredited and its programs are recognized by traditional schools and employers, ensuring you receive usable credits or credentials.

✦

The choice of school for your child is important academically, emotionally, and socially. But it is also a financial decision. According to the College Board, the national average for community college tuition in 2012 was $3,000 per year or $10,000 if you include room, board, and fees. The average state college or university cost $17,860 for tuition, fees, room, and board. Lastly, the average private school cost $39,500 per year, although some cost more than $60,000. If we limit the time in school to four years starting in 2012 and assume no tuition increases during that time (an impossible outcome) for the purposes of this comparison, combining 2 years in a community college living at home with 2 years at a state college or university would average $41,720. Going to a state college or university for 4 years would average $71,440, while going to a private college or university for 4 years would average $158,000. And this is just for one child.

Costs are different in each state. But the cost difference of the various options is always immense. With three children, *higher education could easily cost an American family from $150,000 to $720,000.* No one knows what this will cost in the future, although one online 529 Plan Calculator estimates 4 years at an elite private college for *one* child born in 2012 will cost $523,665! It is hard to imagine many parents being able to afford that, no matter how much incomes rise by 2033.

PAYING THE BILL BY PUTTING IT OFF

At today's cost, many families are unable to pay for post-secondary education, even with savings, money available from parents' current incomes, and scholarships. As a result, many pay part of the cost by getting *student loans.* According to the federal Department of

Education, in 2012 the average American college student graduated with a debt of $26,000 (up from $24,000 two years earlier). Meanwhile, private and for-profit school graduates often owe $50,000 or more, with some owing $100,000. And this is just for an undergraduate education. In fact, *education loans are now the second largest debt category for Americans.* So it is important to understand the unique nature of these loans.

Governments recognize the value of having an educated population. Aside from sponsoring 529 Plans and providing partial scholarships for in-state students, the tuition charged to in-state students at state schools is much less than the real cost of educating a student. Meanwhile, the federal government provides student loans (*Stafford Loans) and* guarantees to banks to offer student loans at reduced rates, while colleges and universities use some of their endowment or income to provide loans to students, along with partial scholarships and on-campus part-time jobs. And lastly, if 529 Plans, parental help, scholarships, and the above loans and jobs are not enough, students can get non-guaranteed loans from banks at higher interest rates. Luckily, even students with some higher-cost bank loans pay a low average interest rate for their "basket" of loans.

Students use the loans they receive to pay college expenses, with most of the money going directly to schools (a great source of income for them) for tuition, supplies, room, and board. Under current rules, students do not begin paying back these loans until six months after leaving "full-time student status" or graduating, whichever comes first. And, no interest is charged on most student loans until repayment begins. If a person returns to school, he or she makes no payments while in school and interest on the loans does not keep accumulating. Thus, while their old loans are in suspended animation, students may get new loans to pay for continuing their studies.

No other loan consumers get such a good deal. Nevertheless, when students leave school, the impending onset of loan payments makes it important to find a job quickly. This is not always easy. According to 2012 federal Department of Labor statistics, 48% of recent college graduates are unemployed or underemployed. Given this situation, in 2013 Congress agreed to keep student loan interest rates low in the short-run. However, if interest rates are allowed to rise or the six-month waiting period before payments begin or the suspension of interest while students are in school are eliminated in the next few years, as has been suggested by some members of Congress, students will be under even more pressure to find jobs when they leave school and will pay a higher price for returning to school.

Here is how repayment works. As with car loans and mortgages, most of early student loan payments go to interest. And the total amount owed is divided into equal monthly payments, traditionally over a term of 10 years. Given this relatively short term and the large amounts involved, *monthly payments can be quite large*, making it difficult for many people to keep up with their payments. In fact, economists are warning a student loan crisis is on the horizon that may cause personal bankruptcies at a rate rivaling home foreclosures and medical bills.

In response to this dilemma, banks, colleges, and governments now offer more flexible repayment plans, some of which last 25 years. While this reduces monthly payments, it increases the total amount to be paid back. Other plans feature low initial payments that increase over time or with a balloon payment at the end of the term. These plans are based on the assumption that as former students age, their incomes increase, making it easier to pay higher loan payments. But given the employment uncertainty facing many adults today and that other expenses are certain to rise over the years, *it is far better to make equal payments throughout the term of the loan*. So, if monthly payments are too high, it makes sense to choose a longer repayment period. Finally, the crippling effect of student loans often makes it necessary for parents to pay part or all of their children's student debt, with this one financial responsibility delaying retirement for some parents.

As with mortgages, making an extra payment each year shortens the term and reduces the total payback amount of a student loan. But if you have that "extra" money, it may be better to put it in a retirement savings plan. After all, most investments achieve higher rates of return than the interest rate paid on student loans. If, however, student loan interest rates go up or you decide to make extra payments to limit the psychological burden of having student loans, be sure to *accelerate payments on the loans with the highest interest rates first.*

Given the student loan payment crisis, the Obama administration has proposed that total payments for federal government loans and government guaranteed bank loans should be limited to 10% of "disposable" income (money left after paying for essentials like food, housing, health care, etc.). And existing loans should be consolidated at a lower interest rate than that charged on the old loans, mirroring the refinancing of mortgages. Since it would take a *very* long time to pay off these loans, those who make all payments on time for 20 years would have the remainder of their debt cancelled. For those who work in public service or for not-for-profit organizations, the debt might even be cancelled after 10 years. Hence, *if* this program is enacted, former students would have the unique ability to lower their monthly payments without increasing their total payback amounts.

✦

Each family needs to be realistic about their finances and their child's educational options. Since a former student's income plays a large role in one's ability to make loan payments, many financial experts recommend picking schools and programs that *limit total student debt to no more than the starting annual salary of the job a student is planning (and hoping) to get after graduation.*

Despite the way the above discussion applies to most students,

students from poor families who receive full scholarships may attend any school that makes that offer. For those who do not receive full scholarships and those with *slightly* more family means, the community college to public college or university route makes perfect sense. So, while it is not easy, children with limited means *can* get a good education in America.

For middle-class students, state *and* private schools are good choices. While it is seldom acknowledged, schools are "selling" two products: preparation for a career and adulthood, *and* a credential that creates job and social opportunities. Fairly or not, private schools offer connections few public schools can match. There are, however, exceptions. Some private colleges charge top dollar but do not improve a student's employability or income prospects. They are elite in cost alone. Meanwhile, some state universities have elite national reputations, while others rank among the best in the nation in certain areas of study. People in industries associated with those fields fully value those state school credentials. Lastly, for students who plan on "staying local" as adults, a larger number of state and private schools have great reputations within their local regions.

It is also worth noting that students may get enough scholarship help from private schools to make the out-of-pocket cost and loan burden only slightly higher than for state schools, which seldom have as much money to give out. As a teacher I often counseled parents to wait for "final offers" before their child chose a school. After all, when comparing costs, all that matters is the *net* cost of going to one school versus another.

Finally, there is a growing feeling among some parents and children that the cost of a college education or the debt incurred while getting one are no longer justified by the income benefits of a college degree. While it is true that new graduates over the last 5 years have faced a weak job market and found it difficult to capitalize on their educational accomplishments, this will not be true for college graduates in the long run. In our society, life-time earnings still reflect educational accomplishments and connections. And they always will. In any case, it is important to remember that the biggest benefit of receiving a good education is not financial: it changes a person in ways that are useful in all aspects of life. So, a quality education is still a good investment.

CREDIT CARDS

The third largest source of consumer debt is bank-issued credit cards. Credit cards allow people to do their daily business without using cash, checks, or debit cards. However, *credit card interest rates are among the highest consumers pay*. And if a credit card is used to cover *overdrafts* on a bank account or get *cash advances*, interest is even higher and starts the day of the transaction instead of the due date of the next payment. As a result, even if the debt is paid "on time," interest is charged for these transactions.

If everyone only used credit cards for purchases and paid the full amount on time each month, banks would lose money on their credit card business, despite the transaction fees retailers pay for processing card purchases and the annual fees consumers pay for some cards. But this is not what happens. Millions of Americans carry balances forward from month to month while running up new debts. This is very profitable for banks, but a disaster for consumers. Without limiting purchases to those that can be paid for within the next month and making *full* payments on time, there is no chance a consumer will stay out of debt, keep up with other financial needs, or have a good credit rating when it is needed for important purchases like a home or a car.

Acting responsibly in this realm is not easy. Credit card companies constantly offer cards to people who lack the means or discipline to handle credit, young people with little income or credit history, and those with significant debts on other cards. Credit card statements also list a *minimum payment*, as if paying that amount will keep the cardholder out of trouble. Nothing could be further from the truth. If the minimum is paid each month, it takes years to pay off the debt and interest is added on the remaining balance, including previously charged interest, every month along the way. Lastly, credit cards come with a *spending limit* that increases if the card is used a lot. Many people interpret this limit as a measure of how much they can afford to borrow. Not true. This is just the card company's way of encouraging consumers to spend *up* to that amount, even if it is more than they can handle. In any case, given the constant encouragement to "spend your way to a better life" by credit card companies and retailers, few people can resist the urge to use a piece of plastic that makes it seem as if they are not spending "real" money when they shop.

Given this situation, it is important to *comparative shop for a credit card* like you would for any other product. Some cards charge annual fees but low interest rates for unpaid balances. Others charge higher interest rates but no annual fee. There is also a confusing array of "rewards" programs. Some cards offer cash back, while others offer merchandise or gift certificates for retail outlets, the option of turning reward points into airline tickets, special customer service, or reduced prices for travel. Only you can decide which benefits and costs fit the way you use credit cards.

If credit cards are handled responsibly, they can be a useful "tool." But credit cards can become an addiction that ruins a person's life. Some people need counseling to learn how to manage credit card use while others have to give up credit cards entirely. Put simply, *everyone should think of credit cards and credit in general as a tool of convenience, not as an invitation to act as if you have more income than you really do.*

OTHER CONSUMER DEBTS

Many businesses and stores offer their own credit cards. Some come with discounts such as "5% off your first day's purchase" or "3% off every time you use our card in our store." Others come with special arrangements for paying, such as "no money down and no interest for 1 year." However, all have very high interest rates, even when compared to "bank-logo" credit cards.

Stores understand that giving a consumer a card with the store's name on it creates a more loyal customer who will spend more in that store than he or she would with any other method of payment. To enhance this effect, stores periodically offer their card holders coupons or special discounts. These may amount to real savings. But *no matter how good a sale is, if you can't afford what you are spending, it is a bad deal.* Moreover, store cards are actually issued by banks as a way for the bank to reach people who are shoppers while charging them even higher interest rates.

Before accepting these cards, a consumer should ask "what are the risks of this arrangement for me?" First, one "red flag" credit rating agencies use is excessive numbers of credit cards. So, it is not a good idea to let 5% off purchases, coupons, or "private" sales jeopardize your credit scores or cause you to spend more than you should. Therefore, you should only accept a store credit card if it provides extra savings on things you can afford and would buy from that store anyway. Above all, everyone should limit total credit card purchases to what can be paid by the due date each month. This will *eliminate interest on credit card debt from monthly expenses*, a change that would greatly help most people stay on a budget and have enough money to save for retirement.

Second, people who purchase an appliance, furnace, furniture, television, or computer with "no money down" or "no interest" for a period should read the fine print in the credit agreement carefully. In many deals, payments must be made during the interest-free period. And the entire purchase must be paid for by the end of the "no interest" period. If not, interest is added to the *entire* purchase price back to the day it was bought at a very high interest rate. This is true even if most of the purchase cost has already been paid. So, be sure the monthly payments fit into your budget and you pay off the entire loan on time. If you mess up on this one, you pay a big penalty.

PERSONAL LOANS: FAMILY AND FRIENDS TO THE RESCUE

There are times when family and friends lend money to help pay for medical or other bills, a car, or a down payment on a house. These *private loans* come in all sizes and arrangements. Some require repayment of the principal but no interest. Others charge interest at a lower rate than what the borrower could get from any other source. Some come with fixed repayment schedules, while others allow the borrower to suspend payments for a while with no penalty. Some even cancel the debt if early payments are made on time and in full. In fact, the purpose of private loans is often to help out the borrower with terms that would not be offered by any other loan source.

If you get a personal loan, adhere to its terms. While you might "get away with" things that would never be tolerated by a bank, there is a reason Shakespeare said a friend should "neither a lender nor borrower be." Or, to cite another saying, "if you borrow money from a friend, first decide which you need more: the money or the friend." Also remember there is a big difference between a gift and a loan. In a gift, money is given without expectations of repayment, other probably than gratitude. However, if you *give* large gifts talk to an accountant about the tax rules governing them.

Above all, parties to a private loan or gift should agree on the nature and terms of the help. If it is a gift, what, if anything, is expected in return? If it is a loan, there should be a written agreement about what will be paid back, including interest, and on what schedule. And someone should keep repayment records to avoid later misunderstandings.

As long as you follow these suggestions and no one feels "taken advantage of," getting help in this way is a blessing and should be cause for a deeper relationship between the lender and borrower, no matter what Shakespeare said.

CHAPTER 7

DEATH AND TAXES: BEN FRANKLIN'S TWO CERTAINTIES

Questions: How can I save money when my taxes are so high? Why do people with more income than me pay less tax than I do?

Americans pay many taxes, including income tax; sales tax; Social Security, Unemployment, and Medicare tax (the last three altogether, "payroll taxes"); capital gains tax; gift tax; estate tax; property and school taxes; fuel tax; cigarette and alcohol taxes; highway, bridge, and tunnel tolls; hotel (tourism) taxes; and fees for an array of other activities. Some taxes and fees are levied by the federal government and its agencies, others by state or local governments, and some by two or all three levels of government. Nobody likes paying taxes, but governments need money to deliver services, many of which are essential to everyday life in America.

Despite the universal benefits and complaints that come from taxation, there is no tax equality for Americans. Forgetting for a moment federal taxes, *state and local taxes are much higher in some places than others*. For example, according to the Tax Institute of America, a family living in New York City with a gross income of $150,000 (a benchmark level of the Tax Institute) pays 12.1% of its gross income to local and state taxes, while a similar family living in Phoenix Arizona pays 6.5%. Thus, similar Americans' taxes differ depending on where they live. Given this complicating factor, we will focus here on *federal* income, payroll, gift, and estate taxes, the taxes that most universally affect the ability to amass, hold, and use wealth. But *your* investment strategy and tax planning should reflect your particular federal, state, *and* local tax situation.

INCOME TAX

For most Americans, there are *two income taxes*. One is levied by the federal government and one by their state. However, Washington DC, nine states, and the U.S. territories (Puerto Rico, Guam, Samoa, etc.) have no income tax. While the territories and Washington DC depend on the federal government to cover many of their expenses, the nine states without income taxes rely on sales and other taxes and fees to pay for the benefits and services they provide to their residents.

To make things even more complicated, the states that have income taxes use different rules and rates for taxing income. For example, thirty-five states use the federal government's definition of *adjusted gross income* (see below), while six states use their own calculations. Some tax interest and dividend income while others do not. And lastly, some exempt Social Security benefits from taxation, while others tax some or all of it.

FEDERAL INCOME TAX BRACKETS

The United States first instituted an income tax in 1861 as a "temporary" measure to pay for the Union's Civil War effort, simultaneously establishing the Internal Revenue Service (IRS) to collect the tax. After the Civil War, the income tax lapsed before being reinstituted in 1894 with a flat rate of 2% for every taxpayer. In 1896, the U.S.

Supreme Court ruled the income tax unconstitutional except during wartime. But in 1906, the 16th Amendment to the U.S. Constitution gave Congress the power to levy a "direct" income tax. In 1913 this led to the issuing of 1040 Tax Forms, which listed four tax rates (1%, 2%, 3%, and 4%) for different income levels and expenses that could be deducted from income before calculating tax owed. This made our income tax system *progressive* (progressing in steps) by defining *tax brackets* that were meant to ensure low income earners would pay a smaller percentage of their income as tax than high income earners.

1040 Tax Forms were first used to collect taxes during World War I and have been used ever since. But over the years, tax brackets have been adjusted in four ways. First, Congress has periodically changed the number of brackets. Second, it has changed the *percentage* of income paid as tax in each bracket. Third, the top income limit of each bracket has been adjusted in response to inflation. And fourth, there are now *three categories of tax filers*. Single filers who are *not* heads of a household have *six tax brackets*; single filers who *are* heads of households have a second set of six brackets; and joint filers, two people who file as a single entity, usually a married couple, have a third set of six brackets. *The purpose of this system is to allow those with greater financial responsibility more income within each percentage of tax paid*. For example, joint filers are allowed twice the income of a single filer who is not the head of a household in each of the lower brackets. Here are the tax brackets and rates for 2012 for joint tax filers.

CHART 7-1: 2012 JOINT FILERS TAX BRACKETS FOR "TAXABLE INCOME:"

Range of Income	Bracket Name and Tax Percentages Paid
$0 - $17,700	10% Bracket: pay 10% on all taxable income
$17,701 - $70,700	15% Bracket: pay 10% on first $17,700 of income and 15% on the rest
$70,701 – $142,700	25% Bracket: pay 10% on first $17,700, 15% on next $53,000, and 25% on the rest
$142,701 - $217,450	28% Bracket: pay 10% on first $17,700, 15% on next $53,000, 25% on next $72,000, and 28% on the rest
$217,451 - $388,350	33% Bracket: pay 10% on first $17,700, 15% on next $53,000, 25% on next $72,000, 28% on next $74,750, and 33% on the rest
$388,350 – unlimited*	35% Bracket: pay 10% on first $17,700, 15% on next $53,000, 25% on next $72,000, 28% on next $74,750, 33% on next $170,900, and 35% on the rest

*__Note__: For households with incomes of $450,000 or more, the percentage paid as tax has been raised for 2013 and beyond. This will create a seventh tax bracket.

Before defining "taxable income," let's pause to briefly examine the concept of tax brackets. As illustrated in Chart 7-1, a household with a *taxable* income of $175,000 is at the midpoint of the 28% bracket. But only $32,300 of that income is taxed at the 28% rate. The rest is taxed 10%, 15%, and 25%. Since we only pay our tax bracket's rate on the last, or marginal, dollars of our taxable income, tax brackets are often called *marginal tax brackets*.

FROM "GROSS" TO "TAXABLE," THE GAME OF DISAPPEARING INCOME

Our graduated tax structure is a remarkably simple system for sharing the financial burden for federal services and programs in a way meant to leave the maximum number of people with enough money to live a reasonably good life. But that is far from the whole story. As implied above, *taxable income is not the same as gross income*. In fact, every taxpayer has *three "incomes." Gross income* is all the money made in a year, whatever its source. *Adjusted gross income* is the income left after reducing the amount by taking *personal deductions*. And lastly, *taxable income* is the amount left after eliminating special categories of income and subtracting tax deductions and tax credits. By the time this process of "disappearing income" is finished, taxable income, the figure that determines a taxpayer's tax bracket and the amount of tax to be paid, is much lower than gross income for all middle- and high-income taxpayers.

Given this opportunity to lower *your* tax bill, let's take a look at some of the ways Americans reduce their taxable income in relation to their gross income.

First, all taxpayers get a *personal deduction*. Joint filers get two. If there are other *dependents* in the family, usually children or elderly parents, there are deductions for each dependent. Once these deductions are taken, the remaining income is the taxpayer's *adjusted gross income*.

Second, there is an array of *tax deductions and credits*. This is done by the government to acknowledge the necessity or importance of particular expenses, or to encourage taxpayers to spend money in certain ways by giving them a tax break when they do so.

Let's start with deductions. For some deductions taxpayers may subtract actual (*itemized*) expenses only if they spend more than a certain amount or percentage of their adjusted gross income. For example, if joint filers had 2012 charitable donations that exceeded $11,600, they could deduct the itemized amount. Or, if they spent more than 7.6% of adjusted gross income on health costs, some of those costs were deductible. However, for other categories of spending, the tax filer may deduct itemized expenses no matter how much or little was spent. For example, interest paid on a mortgage or student loan is usually deductible.

Turning to health-related deductions, the two most common

are *Flexible Spending Accounts (Flex Plans) and Health Savings Accounts (HSAs),* which can only be established by an employer. Money set aside by an employee in these plans does not count as taxable income and can be used for child care, medical costs, or eldercare. But if the employee doesn't spend money in a Flex Plan or HSA, he or she loses it, which may eliminate the advantage gained by the tax deduction. That being said, when an employee *does* spend money in these plans, there is a significant saving. For example, an employee who spends $100 in a Flex Plan only has to earn $100 of *gross* income to fund that expense. Meanwhile, a person in the 15% bracket without a Flex Plan must earn $119 to generate $100 of after-tax money to pay for that expense, while a household in the 25% bracket must earn $131 to generate $100.

Property taxes, sales taxes, Social Security and Medicare taxes, accountant and other professional fees may also be deductible.

Self-employed people may *deduct a percentage of business expenses,* including car costs, tolls, gas bills, plane tickets, meeting costs, business meals, capital improvements for the business, and office expenses. If the office is in the owner's home, some of the home's electricity, heating, telephone, and other household bills may be deductible. Business losses and the cost of equipment and buildings used up (*depreciated*) in the course of doing business may also be deducted. For people who are not self-employed, some going-to-work expenses or job supplies may be deductible.

Income earned as dividends or interest from an investment, or from selling property or an investment at a profit, *are not considered taxable income.* They are taxed separately as *capital gains* at a fixed rate (currently 15%), no matter how big they are. One time in life, a homeowner receives an exemption from capital gains tax on a primary residence if it is sold at a profit. This is an added incentive to own a home. Lastly, 529 Educational Savings Plan contributions may be deductible from state income taxes, while growth in a 529

Plan is exempt from all taxes, as is money in a 529 Plan when it is used for higher education.

There are also time-limited *tax credits* for buying energy-efficient home improvements and vehicles. These *directly reduce tax owed*. For example, if the government offers a tax *credit* of $1,000 for a high-efficiency furnace and you buy one for $2,000 during the period covered by the offer, you *subtract $1,000 from the tax you owe*. But if you receive a tax *deduction* of $1,000, you subtract $1,000 from your adjusted gross income. If you are in the 15% tax bracket, this gives you a tax saving of $150. So a tax credit is the most generous benefit the government can give a taxpayer and, not incidentally, the best way for the government to support certain industries.

For those without a lot of deductions, there is a non-itemized *standard deduction*. In practice, a taxpayer deducts either his or her itemized deductions *or* the standard deduction, whichever is greater. Meanwhile, *contributions to pensions and most retirement accounts and returns within those accounts are deductible, whether the tax filer takes the standard deduction or itemizes*. So, those who put money into most retirement plans get the full benefit of the contribution and its growth through the years. These are called *tax deferred accounts* because tax is paid on this money when it is used later. However, there is one retirement account, a *Roth IRA*, in which contributions *are* taxed "up-front." But growth within a Roth is not taxed. Nor is there any tax paid when Roth money is used, as long as the taxpayer is 59½ or older. (Note: Starting in 2014, taxpayers will get a tax *credit* instead of a deduction for contributions to non-Roth retirement accounts, with the eligible credit depending on the tax filer's adjusted gross income.)

Once you receive a Social Security pension, it is partially deductible from your federal adjusted gross income, while some states with income taxes give a tax deduction or credit as well. In states with income taxes, state public employees' and teachers' pensions may be exempt from state taxes. Active military, veterans, former federal employees, and politicians get their own tax advantages. There is also a federal deduction for seniors who have very modest incomes and do not itemize. Finally, inherited and gifted money (see below) may not count as income for the recipient.

✦

High-income households are limited to claiming itemized deductions of no more than 35% of their adjusted gross income. But when taken with tax credits and other accounting maneuvers, many high-income earners pay very little tax in relation to their gross income. To address this situation, in 1969 Congress and President Richard M. Nixon enacted the *Alternative Minimum Tax* (*AMT*). This is how the AMT worked in 2012. Once a joint filer with an adjusted gross income above $72,450 (the *AMT Floor*) listed all income, deductions, and taxes owed under the tax bracket system, that amount was compared to the tax payable on the same adjusted gross income under the AMT. The tax filer then paid the higher amount. In practice, households with incomes modestly above $72,450 rarely paid the AMT amount. But higher earners who had a lot of deductions may have had to pay the AMT amount.

The AMT does not work for high-income households that get most of their income from capital gains or keep money in foreign countries with lower or no income taxes. Nevertheless, the AMT is controversial because many wealthy Americans feel it is unfair for them to pay income tax using different rules than everyone else. Meanwhile, people modestly above the AMT Floor do not feel they are wealthy enough to be treated this way, especially if they live in high-cost areas of the United States. In response, Congress has raised the AMT floor several times over the years, finally establishing an automatic mechanism to index the floor to inflation beginning in 2013.

✦

Under the tax bracket system, deductions and credits can be significant. For example, a household with a gross income of $110,000 that "maxes out" on deductions, credits, and retirement account contributions might have a taxable income of $70,000. This keeps all income in the 10% and 15% brackets. As a result, *a joint-filing family with a gross income of $110,000 and no self-employment income might pay $9,615 to the IRS, a tax rate of 8.8% of gross income, despite being at the top end of the 15% bracket.* However, if this family lives in New York City, they pay $13,310 for payroll, state, and local taxes. This leaves a net income of $87,075. Or if this family lives in Phoenix, its net income is $93,235. Moreover, as this example illustrates, for many American families the federal income tax is less than half their tax burden.

BENEFITS FOR THE POOR

Those with less income do not get the above tax breaks. But they may be eligible for federal, state, and local government assistance programs like *Temporary Assistance for Needy Families* (welfare), the *Low Income Home Energy Assistance Program* (LIHEAP), the *Supplemental Nutrition Assistance Program* (SNAP, formerly called Food Stamps), *Medicaid*, and, in some states, a credit that reduces state income tax paid by renters. Unfortunately, states do not use the same guidelines to qualify residents for federally-sponsored programs, all of which are partially paid for by state and local governments. For example, a household with a single wage-earner, two children, and an income of $5,101 is considered *too wealthy* to qualify for Medicaid in Texas. In Mississippi the Medicaid ceiling for a similar family is $8,200. Meanwhile, Hawaii, Minnesota, Alaska, and Connecticut have the highest ceilings for Medicaid qualification. Here again, similar Americans are treated differently depending on where they live.

Extremely low income earners do not have to file income tax returns at all, while some who have just enough income to file pay no tax. In fact, in 2011, *46% of American households paid no federal income tax*, including seniors, unemployed adults, "the working poor," some veterans and military personnel, and children. Lastly, families that earn just enough to pay income tax qualify for the *Earned Income Tax Credit (EITC)*. At the upper end of the EITC, joint filers with 3 or more children and a taxable income up to $48,362 get a tax credit of $5,666.

However you feel about who benefits most from our income tax system, *you need to claim all legal tax deductions and credits that apply to you, especially those that allow you to save for retirement*. For those with modest incomes, doing this well is an essential tool in the effort to amass wealth.

ESTATE TAXES

Many people hope to leave property and money to their children or other descendants. That is why people write a Will that specifies how their money and other assets will be divided among heirs, and who will be responsible for taking care of minor children. No matter how small your estate, *it is essential for each adult to have a Will,* even if the adults in a family hold property jointly. A lawyer can help you with this task.

If an individual dies without a Will (is *intestate*) a judge decides where that individual's assets go. This often means a large part of the estate goes to taxes and the remainder is divided among heirs without regard for the wishes of the deceased. When an individual *with* a Will dies, the Will is *probated,* a process governed by state law that can be expensive and time consuming. However, if a Will is in good order, taxes may be minimized and the wishes of the deceased are honored. If the estate is left to a spouse, there is no tax owed to the federal government or any state. So other than paying death-related costs or debts, the estate retains its full value. The key question is what happens when an estate is left to others or the second spouse dies.

An estate is defined as assets passing from *an individual* to heirs, including money, stocks, bonds, property, and personal belongings like furniture, antiques, jewelry, and art. In 2013, a joint estate of $10,200,000 held by a married couple could be divided to allow *each* spouse to leave up to $5,100,000 (an amount that is periodically adjusted to reflect inflation) to heirs without *any* federal estate tax. Any amount over this limit is taxed at a rate of 40%.

For Americans with modest incomes, the *federal* definition of a tax-free estate allows the transfer of assets *after* the death of the second spouse to involve no federal tax. For those with larger estates, the federal tax burden is usually minimal. For example, in 2013 an estate of $6,100,000 faced a federal tax of $400,000. So, with proper planning, a married couple could leave an estate of $12,200,000 to heirs with a tax load of $800,000. This amounts to a tax rate of 6.5%, not the apparent 40%. Meanwhile, the *cost base* for property and investments in an estate is re-set at the time of death, erasing any capital gains tax that would have been due on past growth of those assets, a saving that might exceed the entire estate tax bill.

If an estate exceeds the allowed limit, estate taxes may be minimized by creating *Trusts* that hold assets "outside" the estate of either person in the senior generation. Trusts may also simplify the probate process. Under current law, *Insurance Trusts may be created to hold death benefits, shielding that money from estate tax when it is inherited.* Similarly, *Disclaimer Trusts* may be created with other assets by a surviving spouse within nine months of the death of the first spouse. The surviving spouse may even be the sole *Trustee and beneficiary* of a Trust, in which roles he or she may manage the Trust, receive its income, or use its principal to support a "reasonable lifestyle." If assets are sold within a Trust for more than they originally cost, the Trust must pay tax on the difference ("realized gain"). Similarly, money withdrawn from a Trust is taxed as income of the beneficiary. Lastly, when a Trust is set up, *secondary* beneficiaries should be named who will inherit the Trust upon the death of the primary beneficiary. This allows the secondary beneficiaries to receive the Trust's assets without having to pay estate tax on them.

The decision on whether to establish Insurance or Disclaimer Trusts should be governed by the size of the "consolidated" estate held by a surviving spouse and an estimate of what tax laws might be at the time of the surviving spouse's death. This is not an exact science. Congress has changed estate tax laws often and is likely to do so again. As important, some states levy their own estate tax. New York, for example, collects tax on estates over $1,000,000. Thus, *some modest-income earners* in New York amass enough wealth and property to *face a state estate tax*. In addition, each state with an estate tax has its own rate schedule. Clearly, given the complexity of federal estate tax law and the differences in state laws, those with significant estates should consult an accountant and a lawyer on how best to structure their estates and Wills to minimize taxes, now and in the future.

GIFT TAX

Some people do not want to wait until dying before giving some of their wealth to heirs. They would rather give money or property to family members right away. Under current tax rules, *a person can gift up to $14,000 annually (again, a limit that is adjusted periodically) to each of these individuals: child, child-in-law, grandchild, grandchild-in-law, great-grandchild, great-grandchild-in-law, nephew, niece*, and so on. So, depending on how many people are in this group, a person can give away a lot of money each year. The one giving the gift (the *donor*) pays tax on the gifted money as income in that year, but the recipient of the gift pays no tax on that money. There is also a life-time limit of $1,000,000 a donor may give to any one recipient. However, the biggest benefit of gifting is that *gifted money that falls within the* *annual and lifetime limits is not added back into the estate when the donor dies*, which may reduce or eliminate estate taxes.

The estate and gift tax provisions of our tax code allow Americans to transfer a great deal of wealth to heirs with little or no tax. However you feel about the fairness of these rules, one thing is clear. *Those with modest incomes who receive inheritances or gifts may not have to save as much to secure their futures.* If these benefits are large enough, they should invest their money to preserve it with moderate growth. Taking risks to grow their money more quickly should be avoided.

✦

Among the most important lessons in this chapter is *the difference between "pre-tax" and "after-tax" money*. The old saying goes that "a penny saved is a penny earned." But if you are in the 15% bracket and include all taxes owed to various governments, saving an "after-tax" penny (instead of spending it) is equal to earning 1½ cents of "pre-tax" income. If you are in the 25% bracket or higher, you would have to earn 2 cents or more. So, a more accurate saying would be "a penny saved is at least one and a half pennies earned."

In summary, while there is no question taxes diminish a family's annual net income and affect a person's ability to amass, preserve, use, or pass on wealth to heirs, the tax laws also allow people to avoid a portion of their apparent tax burden. There is nothing illegal in this. *Every taxpayer should use the tax laws to maximize, to the best of his or her ability, the means to accumulate enough wealth to sustain a good lifestyle until the end of life.*

CHAPTER 8

INSURANCE FOR LIFE AND DEATH

Questions: What kinds of insurance do I need? How can I afford insurance and still pay my bills and save for the future?

MUCH OF THE ADVICE IN THE PREVIOUS CHAPTERS ASSUMES YOU AND your spouse will be around long enough to secure your futures and provide for those you love. It also assumes your household will earn a consistent living and that the last period of life will not drain your resources, leaving no money for your final days or for your spouse if he or she survives you.

HEALTH INSURANCE

Aside from bouts of unemployment, the greatest threat to the above assumption is a health crisis. Despite current arguments about access to health insurance or the means to pay for it, that is why there is a general understanding in the United States of the need for health insurance. While it is seldom seen in this light, *health insurance is a financial tool.* For a breadwinner, homemaker, or family child-care provider, or someone who is all three, access to medical care is a protection of the ability to provide services to his or her family and society. Without health insurance, a health crisis may lead to a family's immediate economic ruin or, for those who can bear the initial costs, ongoing prescriptions, therapies, care, or loss of income or free childcare may have the same effect over time. That is why *medical bills are the number one cause of personal bankruptcy in America.*

EMPLOYMENT-BASED POLICIES

Many people receive health insurance through work. With *employment-based policies,* the employer pays part or all of the *premiums,* making health care more affordable for the employee's entire family. These policies are priced according to a contract between the employer and a local health insurance company or Health Maintenance Organization (HMO), the first of which was organized by Kaiser Steel for its employees in Oakland California in 1945. By analyzing the average age, habits, and health risks associated with work done by members of the group, the HMO or insurance company is able to offer insurance at lower premiums than they offer to the general public. After all, most employee groups have relatively low risks of incurring medical expenses because they do not include chronically ill people who are unable to work, the elderly (except for retirees, who are shunted off to Medicare after age 65), and extremely poor individuals, the demographic categories most prone to high medical bills.

These advantages are currently eroding. Some employers no longer offer any health insurance, while others are cutting back on their contributions to premiums. Meanwhile, HMOs and insurance companies are cutting back on the medical services that are covered *and* increasing *co-payments* (*co-pays*) patients pay when they use services that are covered. As a result of the skyrocketing cost of medical services and the need for profit by insurance companies, premiums have also risen much faster than the rate of inflation.

To make health insurance more affordable, many employers offer Flex Plans to house pre-tax money for co-pays and services that are not covered by insurance. Employers may also offer health insurance policies that require the insured to pay a fairly large amount (*deductible*) before the insurance "kicks in." To cover the deductible, employers may offer Health Savings Accounts (HSAs), into which employees can deposit pre-tax money. These "*high-deductible*" *policies* usually have low premiums but high co-pays. So, these plans are only less expensive for relatively healthy families.

NON-EMPLOYMENT OPTIONS

Despite the higher costs facing employees, employment-based coverage is still a bargain. Without it, the options are limited and much more expensive. First, some business groups and professional associations offer group health insurance to their members. These plans usually cover less than employment-based plans and have higher premiums, co-pays, *and* deductibles. But they offer some pricing advantages by spreading the insurance company's risk across a group of reasonably healthy individuals. Or second, a person or family can purchase an *individual* plan from a local HMO or insurance company. Unfortunately, this is seldom affordable for middle-class families, including the self-employed. (Note: Some organization and individual plans are disappearing as insurance is offered through "health care exchanges" set up under the 2010 Affordable Care Act.)

Despite these options, many Americans have been unable to get health insurance at all because of "pre-existing medical conditions." For these people, the only option has been an employment-based plan that guarantees all employees coverage. That is why the Affordable Care Act prohibits insurance companies and HMOs from denying coverage based on pre-existing conditions, although this provision does not guarantee an individual will be able to afford that coverage.

For Americans unable to afford any health insurance, *Medicaid*, a federal program funded by federal, state, and local governments, provides basic medical coverage, although, as we have seen, each state decides the income ceiling for Medicaid qualification for its residents. For those with too much income to qualify for Medicaid but too little to afford private insurance, some states offer public insurance plans that cover basic medical services for relatively low premiums. The best of these are in Massachusetts and Hawaii. Unfortunately, many state-offered policies are only available for children or young adults, while older individuals may only be allowed to buy them for one or two years. Nevertheless, public plans provide coverage for major health crises and some protection against using up savings. (Note: Some people have too much income to qualify for Medicaid in their state but are not eligible for an Affordable Care Act subsidy because the federal system was based on the assumption those people would receive Medicaid. For these individuals, the new system has done nothing to solve their health insurance problem in a way that is affordable.)

People over 65 who have no other health insurance qualify for *Medicare* Part A, a federal program that provides free basic health care. Seniors may also purchase Medicare Part B from the federal government for a wider range of medical services. The premiums for Part B are deducted from Social Security checks. This coverage may be further improved by buying a *supplemental policy* (also called "top-up insurance" or Parts C and D) from an HMO or private insurance company. These policies cover a wider range of medical services and most prescription costs. But they are only available to those who purchase Part B. Premiums for Parts C and D are paid directly to the insurance company. Lastly, some insurance companies offer an alternative: all-inclusive *Advantage Plans* that have much lower premiums because the federal government rebates a large part of the premium to the insurance company. The government does this because it no longer has to pay claims under Medicare's Part A and

Part B. However, Advantage Plans have higher co-pays and cover fewer services, so people with these plans may not save money if they use a lot of medical services. (Note: Starting in 2014, government subsidies to Advantage Plan premiums will be reduced, which will significantly raise the cost for policyholders.)

Despite all these options, 10% to 15% of Americans (up to 46 million people) currently have no health insurance. Estimates vary, depending on the source. These include a lot of young adults who can't find jobs with health insurance. That is why the Affordable Care Act allows parents to include their children up to age 26 on their policies. Nevertheless, at present, almost a third of Americans are uninsured, underinsured, or financially over-burdened by healthcare costs.

LIFE INSURANCE

The second threat to the ability to support a family and amass wealth is premature death. If this happens to a breadwinner, the family may lose educational options, use up savings, or have to sell their home. If the family's health insurance came from the deceased's employer, there is also a risk of losing that coverage or the ability to afford other health insurance. If the deceased is the primary childcare giver or homemaker in the family, there are other consequences beyond the emotional loss. Services that were provided free are no longer available. This alone can severely affect a family's budget. Lastly, funeral and other costs such as taxes, legal bills, and paying off debts as part of settling an estate may drain a family's savings.

Most people don't like to think about their own death or plan for it. This is a pity because there is an inexpensive product that addresses this threat: *life insurance*. Unfortunately, most Americans see life insurance as "optional." If they can fit it into their budget, fine. If not, they'll go without it or buy too little of it. But if you have people who financially rely on your presence (your family and perhaps business partners), you should have life insurance that names them as beneficiaries to ensure they will be able to continue living a similar life after your death.

TERM INSURANCE

The least expensive life insurance is a *term policy* in which coverage is *rented* for a specific amount of time (term) and *death benefit,* the money paid to the *beneficiaries* listed on the policy when the policyholder dies. While a person applying for a term policy must provide medical information and take a medical exam, most people qualify for coverage at some cost. And, when the term ends, the policyholder has the right to renew the policy without taking new exams or answering medical questions. So if the policyholder's health has gotten worse, he or she still qualifies. However, the policyholder will pay a higher premium for the next term because there is probably less time left to pay premiums before the insurance company has to pay the death benefit.

Those who purchase a term policy when they are young get a 10 to 20 year term with a fixed premium. But those who are older when they first rent coverage must renew their policy every 5 years. No matter when coverage begins, those with habits or pre-existing medical conditions that may shorten their lives pay a higher premium than others their age and gender. After all, they are likely to pay fewer premiums before the company pays the death benefit.

There are three additional things you need to know about term life insurance.

First, paying premiums buys nothing other than a promise from the insurance company to pay the death benefit. Paid premiums do not sit in an account that can be used to pay future premiums or cover other expenses. In insurance terms, premiums create no *cash value*. So if you stop paying premiums, you lose coverage and get nothing back from your previous payments.

Second, beneficiaries pay no income tax on the money they receive when the policyholder dies. So the entire death benefit is available to replace the covered person's economic value. This is one of the great advantages of life insurance. For those with large estates, the establishment of Insurance Trusts also protects death benefits from incurring estate taxes.

And third, while a term policy may be renewed over and over, the policy lapses at age 70½. To get coverage past that age, a term policy must be *converted* to a *whole life policy* (see below). Purchasing a whole life policy before turning 70½ to eventually replace a term life policy is called buying a *wrap-around policy*. However, some whole life policies also expire in your 90s.

Before renewing a term life policy or buying wrap-around insurance, remember why you got life insurance in the first place: to protect others in the event of your death. If you have paid off your mortgage, finished raising children, and done a good job saving, your assets may be adequate to provide your loved ones with what you would have given them if you had lived to a very old age. In that case, you could keep just enough life insurance to pay taxes, debts, funeral, and legal bills at the time of your death, obligations that would otherwise fall to your estate or heirs.

The key is to *only rent as much life insurance as you need and only for as long as you need it*. For example, a person earning $50,000 a year might rent $1,000,000 of coverage. If that person dies in the near future, the $1,000,000 could be invested. With a return of 5% per year, it would generate an annual income of $50,000, replacing the lost income without using up the $1,000,000. Or, the beneficiary could take a smaller amount at first in order to allow the fund to grow. Then the beneficiary could slowly increase the income taken from the fund, keeping up with inflation and the raises the deceased person might have gotten if still alive. Of course, there is also the possibility (and hope) the insured person will *not* die in the near future. In that case, his or her income will probably increase over time, making $1,000,000 of coverage inadequate. So, since buying more insurance later would be much more expensive, a person earning $50,000 should probably rent at least $1,500,000 of coverage from the beginning.

While it is easy to calculate the amount of life insurance a wage earner should rent, it is harder to put a value on work done by a childcare provider or homemaker. But it is important to cover the cost of someone else doing those jobs. For example, if it would cost $25,000 a year to pay someone to perform similar services, it makes sense to purchase a term policy on the childcare provider or homemaker for $400,000 to $500,000. In the event of death, that money could be invested and generate enough income to pay for those services. Since these services are usually only needed during child-rearing years, there is no need to buy "extra" insurance to cover the distant inflated cost of those services. In fact, some of this fund should last beyond the period in which those services are required, with leftover money later used for education, other expenses, or retirement. Moreover, if the covered person *doesn't* die during the child-raising period, the policy could be cancelled or reduced when the need disappears.

Once you reach retirement age, you may have no debts and significant assets and income, some of which may be transferable to your spouse after you die. And you may no longer have earned income that needs to be replaced. If you reach this point, you may safely lower the amount of your term life insurance or let it lapse completely.

WHOLE LIFE INSURANCE

The other products offered by life insurance companies are *whole life, universal, and variable policies*. These include *life insurance coverage and a savings component*, and are mostly sold to young adults with little children. Insurance agents emphasize the idea that these policies "kill two birds with one stone." The covered person gets a death benefit and is "forced" to save money, creating a *cash value* in the policy that can be tapped to pay future premiums, cover emergency expenses, or generate retirement income.

For those who think they lack the discipline to save on their own, this seems like a good idea. But because of fierce competition among insurance companies in the last few years, term life insurance premiums have declined dramatically. According to an on-line service that prices policies from many companies, in September 2012 a non-smoking 32-year-old male in good health could get $1,000,000 of coverage from a top-rated insurance company for $672 per year. Because of longer life expectancy, a woman of similar description got an even lower premium. And these premiums were guaranteed for 20 years. Meanwhile, a whole life policy with a death benefit of $1,000,000 would have cost the same 32-year-old male $9,600 per year, an annual difference of $8,938.

Where does this $8,938 go? Some goes to a higher initial premium for the life insurance. After all, the company will never be able to raise the premium as it can with a term policy. For the first 3 years, the rest of the extra money goes to fees and commissions, a real incentive for the insurance agent and company to recommend this product. So the policyholder loses out on those years of saving and compound interest, years we have already seen have a huge effect on eventual savings. After that, the insurance company invests the savings part of the premium, with the principal and return staying in the policy's savings account. But the company charges fees for these services. Thus, the policyholder has huge up-front costs and never actually saves $8,938 in any year. Furthermore, according to several neutral online research sites, in 2012 the average whole life policy only returned 2.6% on its savings, universal plans averaged 4.2%, and variable plans, which were new and allowed to invest in mutual funds, averaged 7%.

Given the likelihood of outperforming insurance company investment results, no one should purchase a whole, universal, or variable life policy. *The best strategy* is simple. *Rent a term policy and learn to save without the insurance company's help.* Purchase only as much coverage as you need for the period you need it. And buy separate policies for each member of the family whose economic value would have to be replaced in the event of death. In the long run, you will come out far ahead with this strategy.

LONG-TERM CARE INSURANCE

The third threat to your financial plan is *becoming so incapacitated or frail*, especially at the end of life, you will require *long-term medical or nursing care*. As difficult as it is for people to plan for death, it is apparently even harder for them to think about no longer being able to take care of themselves. Perhaps this is because most young adults view this possibility as being very distant and too unpleasant to contemplate. So, few people purchase insurance against that possibility, even though the American Insurance Institute estimates 50% of Americans alive today will need long-term care at some point in their lives. In the United States *today*, if that care is delivered in a nursing home it averages $75,000 per year. For Baby Boomers (those born between 1946 to 1964), current estimates suggest that in 2030 over 23 million people will need nursing home care at an average cost of $300,000 per year! For younger people, the costs will be even higher.

Not everyone will need long-term care. Some people are lucky to remain mentally competent and relatively healthy until shortly before death. However, those with debilitating diseases or injuries may spend significant time in nursing homes, other facilities, or require care at home. Depending on how long they need that care, they may run out of money, leaving them dependent on Medicaid or their children, assuming the latter are willing or able to help. Lastly, a surviving spouse might fall into poverty. Luckily, there are two ways to protect against this fate.

The first option is to purchase *long-term care insurance*. This is a very complex product, in part because there are so many versions of it. Some policies set the amount of money provided when care is needed at a portion or all of *today's* cost for nursing home care. Or the amount may be *indexed* using a simple or compound interest rate. For example, if a benefit increases by a simple rate of 5% per year, it will be worth 2.5 times its original amount in 30 years. However, if a benefit is indexed using a compound rate of 5%, it will be worth 4.3 times its original amount.

There are a number of other issues to consider. Some policies only cover services delivered in a nursing home, while others also cover in-home care. This is a far better option for most people and less expensive for everyone concerned. Policies may cover care for 2, 3, or 4 years. Some policies have 3 month *elimination periods*, in this case the gap between care starting and insurance payments beginning, while others have 6 month elimination periods. Luckily, some care is usually covered by health insurance for 90 days. Long-term care policies may also exclude some services completely or define the need for long-term care in more or less restrictive ways. Lastly, some policies are "portable" across state lines while others are not. In any case, the greater the benefits, the longer they will last, and the more flexible the coverage, the higher premiums will be. Policyholders also pay more for simple-rate indexing and even more for compound-rate indexing.

On the plus side, depending on other health costs, long-term care premium payments may be deductible from federal income tax, while states like New York give a tax credit. This is one item governments want you to buy, if only to lower *their* costs as the providers of Medicaid and Medicare. In addition, some states offer public long-term care policies that are inexpensive by private insurance standards. However, the benefits in these plans are more limited and may only be used for services delivered in the state issuing the plan.

✦

When a person applies for long-term care insurance, he or she has to give the insurance company complete access to medical records, take a physical exam, and answer questions about habits and health history. If there are any pre-existing medical conditions or recent health issues, the applicant may not qualify for coverage or may have to pay higher premiums than others the same age and gender. And those higher premiums last for the rest of life. People who buy policies when they are young and healthy, of course, pay a lower premium. But they pay that premium for a longer period. Most important, if they put this off, their health may get worse, making long-term care insurance too expensive or impossible to get at all.

Given the uncertainty of how long it might be until care will be needed, which benefits will be used, or how much care will cost at that point, it is extremely difficult to decide when to buy coverage, how much to get, or how to index it. Hence, purchasing a long-term care policy requires careful thought and some help from a trustworthy insurance agent. In practice, many people buy long-term care insurance when they are in their 50s or 60s and see their parents require nursing home care. If they have done well as income-earners and savers, these "middle-agers" can budget for this cost as a permanent expense.

A couple in their late-50s or early-60s that bought policies with a 5% simple indexing of total current costs in 2012 might pay premiums for 30 years, for a life-time cost of $100,000, although the out-of-pocket cost would be less if there are tax savings for paying long-term care premiums. $100,000 is a lot of money. But it is only $25,000 more than the cost of *one* year of nursing home care for one person *today*. In fact, if one spouse needs nursing home care for three years 30 years from now, that person's total premium cost ($45,000 for the woman or $55,000 for the man) might provide as much as $562,500, money that would otherwise have to come out of the couple's savings. And, if *both* spouses need 3 years of care, the two policies could cover $1,125,000! While, amazingly, this would probably not cover all expenses if nursing home care is needed for that long, it would make the cost more manageable, greatly reducing the loss of savings. However, it is important to note that if a policyholder dies without using up his or her benefits, those benefits cannot be transferred to a surviving spouse. So each individual needs a separate policy.

The second way to avoid losing savings if long-term care is needed is for parents to *put their assets in their children's names*, with an understanding that those assets or the income derived from them will be used to take care of the parents until both die, with any left-over assets going to heirs as per the parents' instructions. After a waiting period, this allows the parents to qualify for Medicaid coverage for nursing home costs. This preserves some of their estate so it can be used by a spouse or heirs after one parent enters a nursing home. However, this option requires a very trusting relationship with one's children (and children-in-law). And the children might have to pay capital gains tax on any asset transferred to them *before* the parents' deaths. There are also strict laws governing "shielding" assets from use for nursing home care. So, consult an attorney before changing ownership of your estate. If you do this, it is important to do it right.

DISABILITY INSURANCE –

The last threat to your financial plan is *losing the ability to work*. Depending on where you work and the kind of work you do, you could lose your income until you recover. Or, worse, you may never earn as much again, or never be able to work at all.

There is no way to fully protect yourself or your loved ones against the financial consequences of becoming disabled. However, in 1956 the federal government added a disability benefit to the Social Security program. Those who are disabled and no longer able to work usually have to fight through a lot of bureaucratic red tape to receive this benefit. But if they win this battle, Social Security provides some replacement income starting at any age, in some cases for the rest of life. While not enough to sustain even a modest middle-class lifestyle, these payments help.

Disability insurance can also be purchased by an employer to cover employees. Or an employee may purchase it directly from an insurance company. Policies range widely in cost, depending on age, income to be replaced, riskiness of work done, and coverage included. Most policies pay basic bills, such as those for food, education, mortgage, and cars for a set length of time. However, some policies are structured differently. They pay a fixed benefit until the person returns to work or to a certain age, often 67, whichever comes first. Many of these policies pay 45% to 60% of current income tax free for that length of time. While this does not sound like much, it is worth 55% to 75% of a person's pre-disability income, which would have been taxed as earned income.

Disability policies are designed to pay for costs that are *not* covered by health insurance until a person returns to work or earns an income in another way. In other words, *disability insurance is insurance for a person's paycheck, which has the secondary benefit of protecting his or her savings during a disability crisis*. Of course, once a person retires and has no paycheck to protect, there is no need for disability insurance. Lastly, like long-term care insurance, disability insurance is a product with many options. Some have long elimination periods, in this case the time after the onset of a disability before payments begin. Some define disability in different ways, with lump-sum payments for listed losses (fingers, hands, feet, etc.). There are also services that may or may not be covered, as well as differing payment schedules for services that do qualify. That is why it is important to get quotes from several insurance companies and consult a trustworthy insurance agent before selecting the product that best suits your needs.

✦

In summary, *you should do all you can to have health insurance and life insurance. Long-term care and disability insurance are more debatable products*: some experts recommend them while others do not.

The key is to not automatically buy every kind of insurance, or to buy more insurance than you need or the wrong kind of insurance. However, you should not ignore the risks the different kinds of insurance are meant to address. Do your homework and weigh your options. Then make a decision. If necessary, find a way to fit premiums into your annual budget. As with having adequate car, homeowner's, or renter's insurance, this will help you sleep better at night.

CHAPTER 9

GETTING TO THE RETIREMENT STARTING LINE

Questions: How do I know how much I should save each year? How can I save anything or develop a financial plan if I can't even make an annual budget or keep to one I have made?

WE ARE NOW READY TO TACKLE THE ISSUE THAT MOTIVATED THE writing of this book: amassing the resources needed to have an adequate income after retirement. Since designing and carrying out a savings and financial plan is a very personal matter, the remaining chapters will be structured as a personal conversation between you, the reader, and me. We will begin with *non-savings based retirement income*. Then we will turn to the *savings* you will need when you retire. To do this, we must answer five questions:

- How much annual gross income will you need *after* you retire?
- How much retirement income will come from non-savings sources?

- What is the target number for the savings needed to generate enough income from this source after retirement?
- How many years will you have in which to save *before* retiring?
- How much should you save *each year* to reach your savings goal by the time you retire?

PRE-RETIREMENT VERSUS POST-RETIREMENT INCOME

During your income earning years, you are likely to have the greatest financial responsibilities of your life. You may have mortgage payments, property and school taxes, and high going-to-work costs for clothes, transportation, meals, and supplies. You may be saving for education or actively paying education bills. You may be responsible for health insurance and medical bills for four or more people, all of whom have to be fed, taken on vacation, entertained, and clothed. You are likely to have insurance on your home, car(s), life, and perhaps disability. Someone in your family may be paying union dues. And you should be saving money for emergencies and retirement.

During the income earning years, you are also likely to have the highest tax burden in your life. The majority of your taxable income is probably earned income. So you are likely to pay the maximum tax rate for your level of income. In the most active period of life, you pay more government fees and sales tax. Lastly, you pay Social Security, Medicare, and Unemployment (altogether, payroll) taxes.

Luckily, *some expenses diminish after you retire*. You no longer pay union dues or going-to-work costs. If you are an "empty-nester," your family shrinks. Some of your income will not be taxed, especially if you have money in Roth IRAs and get Social Security benefits. If you have less income, a higher percentage of it will be taxed at a lower rate. You may put less money into investment accounts. You may get senior discounts on hotel rooms, restaurant meals, property taxes, and entertainment. Your mortgage may be paid off. Once you have little or no earned income, you will pay less or no payroll taxes. And finally, you may have no education costs.

However, *a few costs may increase after retirement*. With less responsibility for others and more time on your hands, you may travel more, remodel your home, or spend money on adult children or grandchildren. Early in retirement, you may have increased life insurance costs. And your health care costs are almost certain to be higher later in life.

You should consider all these changes when estimating the income you will need after retirement. In one seminar I attended before retiring, financial experts explained that in New York State a retired teacher with 80% of pre-retirement *gross* income has the same *net* (after-tax) income as before retirement. Since some expenses diminish after retirement, this gives that teacher *more* disposable income than before. This matches a recent national survey of financial planners that reported *it takes 70% to 80% of final pre-retirement gross income to maintain a similar lifestyle in the first year of retirement.*

Given these variables, as you near retirement you and your spouse should ask yourselves *"how do we want to live in retirement"* and *"how much will it cost us to do so."* These are tough questions to answer. After projecting what our net income would be at different gross income levels after retirement, I approached this question from a different angle by committing my wife and myself to 82% of our final pre-retirement income for a period that would include one full tax year. I picked 82% because I knew this was attainable for us without cutting into our savings and I was confident this level of income would allow us to do everything we wanted to do in year-1 of retirement and still contribute 3% to our savings, with the goal of our savings keeping up with inflation in the early years of retirement. If the experts were right, we could adjust our income slightly downward later if that became necessary.

After two full years of retirement, we discovered that 82% of our pre-retirement gross income gives us a higher *net* income than before retirement. My Social Security and teacher's pension is partly untaxed. We receive a New York State tax credit for long-term care insurance premiums. And, while our income tax bill is higher than it would be if we were still contributing 8.5% to our savings, it is far smaller than it has been in years.

We also discovered our *net* income goes a lot farther than it would have before retirement. We have no mortgage, going-to-work, or child-raising expenses. We are lucky to have no expenses associated with our parents, other than travel. Our remaining portion of our children's education costs are manageable and will soon disappear. And our long-term care insurance costs will not change for the next 5 years, while our health insurance costs have only increased slightly. If all goes well, I will no longer need life insurance when I reach age 70½, which will save us the cost of those premiums. In the meantime, my wife will qualify for Social Security in less than two years. This will allow us to increase our household income right away or wait in order to increase it by a larger amount later (see below).

Here's the bottom line. With 82% of our previous income, we covered our expenses, contributed 3% to savings, had a little extra money to spend on new items, and our savings grew, despite taking distributions from our savings. This result was achieved during a period in which U.S. stock markets declined and then rebounded to just below their previous levels. In fact, *we could have lived as we did before, saved 3%, and maintained our savings on 77% of our pre-retirement income*. Interestingly, this is near the middle of the range cited in the financial planner survey.

How does this 77% number apply to other people's situations? Let's look at three examples. To maintain their pre-retirement lifestyle and contribute 3% to savings, a household with a final pre-retirement gross income of $100,000 would need an initial retirement income of $77,000. A household with an income of $80,000 would need $61,600. And a household with an income of $50,000 would need $42,500 (not $38,500, since they did not pay a lot of income tax while working). Use these "benchmark" numbers to project your post-retirement income target. But remember, *if you live a long life, you will eventually need a larger income to keep up with inflation*. That is why it is important to have 77% of pre-retirement income, not 74%.

Some expenses continue to diminish as you go through retirement. You may wrap up your financial obligations for education. You will get a senior discount on more goods and services, and perhaps on income and property taxes. In the later years of retirement, you might travel less or be less capable of doing so. Driving less, you might only need one car or use less gas. You may no longer pay life insurance premiums. And lastly, you might sell your home and move to a less expensive one, perhaps in a lower taxed state. In fact, *it is unlikely you will have as expensive a lifestyle at 85 as you have at 65* unless you are in a nursing home or supporting grandchildren or children. To state this in quantitative terms, *the decline in your expenses will lessen the need to keep up with inflation*. So, even though a 3% inflation rate will make it necessary to have $175 in year-20 of retirement to pay for what $100 buys in year-1 of retirement, you are likely to only need $155. Thus, households with a year-1 retirement income of $77,000 will need $119,350; those with a year-1 income of $61,600 will need $95,480; and those with a year-1 income of $42,500 will need $65,870. Use these numbers to project your income needs in year-20 of retirement.

At first glance, these income numbers may seem impossible to achieve. But luckily you are likely to have some *non-savings sources of income*, including Social Security and perhaps a defined-benefit pension, income-producing property, family business, inheritance, or left over rainy-day savings. Some of these incomes may be indexed to inflation. So they will slowly increase after you retire. If you contribute to tax-deferred retirement savings until 70½ and make contributions to Roth IRAs beyond that age, your savings may grow and be able to generate more income later. However, as we will see in Chapter 10, the rules governing tax-deferred accounts will shrink your savings and increase your income tax burden after age 70½.

NON-SAVINGS SOURCES OF INCOME

One of the greatest misunderstandings about retirement planning comes from the fact that some steps you take during your income-earning years will generate a specific amount of monthly or yearly income after retirement, while other steps will generate assets (wealth, in the form of savings, property, belongings, etc.), which will translate into a still unknown amount of income. Moreover, the only calculation that will matter when you get to retirement is having enough income to sustain a desirable lifestyle. In other words, the wealth discussed in the next chapter should only be seen as a means toward an end, with your sole focus on the eventual income your non-savings income and wealth will generate *together*.

Now let's turn to non-savings sources of income for older Americans. The most common non-savings source is *Social Security*. Some people also have defined-benefit pensions and real estate. Once you estimate how much these sources will contribute to your retirement income, you will be able to calculate the income needed from the return on your savings.

SOCIAL SECURITY

Social Security was established in 1935 by Congress and President Franklin Delano Roosevelt as *a guaranteed income program for seniors* who pay into the system while they work. When first enacted, a qualifying senior could take a lump sum payment or a monthly benefit check. The first person to take a lump sum retired in Ohio the day after Social Security began. So he only paid five cents into the system. In return, he received seventeen cents, a 240% return on his contribution! Currently, however, you may only receive monthly benefit checks.

Social Security is the *only* income for many elderly Americans and a significant contributor to the income of most seniors. In fact, *Social Security benefits account for 41% of all income of elderly Americans and replace 40% of pre-retirement income for those who receive them.* In June 2011, there were *54.8 million Americans receiving Social Security,* about 1/6 of the entire American population. It is therefore unlikely Social Security will disappear anytime soon, no matter what some politicians or media personalities suggest. As important, while the *Medicare* Trust Fund *is* running out of money, the Social Security Trust Fund has a surplus and will remain fully solvent until 2033. Nevertheless, it is clear Congress will have to do something to shore up the funding of Social Security after 2033. As a result, there are several cost-cutting changes likely to be enacted in coming years, some of which are already part of Social Security's adjustment mechanism.

First, more of Medicare's cost could be deducted from Social Security, which would shore up the Medicare Trust Fund but leave recipients with less income. This is already happening. Second, Social Security benefits might be taxed more as income or not be as fully indexed to inflation, two "adjustments" that are also already happening. Third, the minimum age for receiving an "early" Social Security benefit (currently 62) might be raised. Fourth, the age for receiving a "full benefit" (presently 66 and already moving to 67 for those born in 1960 or later) could be raised further, as could the age (currently 70) for getting a maximum "delayed" benefit. Fifth, benefits could be lowered to extend the solvency of the Social Security Trust Fund. Sixth, the Social Security tax on earned income or the ceiling for income subject to the tax could be raised, as it has been in recent years. Either change would increase the money coming into the Trust Fund. And lastly, in a more radical move that has been proposed by some politicians and business leaders, contributions to Social Security could be made available to contributors to manage as their own investment accounts. Moreover, if none of these steps are taken, the federal government projects that after 2033 the Trust Fund will only be able to pay 77% of currently scheduled benefits.

✦

Let's take a quick look at how Social Security and other federal benefits are funded, using 2012 numbers that will periodically be adjusted to reflect inflation and income growth. There is a 6.2% Social Security tax on the first $110,100 of an *individual's* annual *earned* income. But no Social Security tax is paid on earned income above $110,100 or on *any* capital gains. There is also a 1.45% Medicare tax on an individual's *entire* earned income. Employers match the employee's Social Security and Medicare taxes, while also paying a small Unemployment tax on the first $7,000 of an employee's earnings. Finally, self-employed people pay all of the above employer *and* employee taxes. Hence, if we count employer contributions, which are really part of an employee's pay (total compensation), for many Americans *Social Security, Medicare, and Unemployment taxes add up to more than their federal income tax burden.*

BENEFITS FOR BABY BOOMERS

Let's look at how people *receive* a Social Security pension benefit.

When Social Security taxes are paid, they go into the *Social Security Trust Fund*. Meanwhile, Medicare and Unemployment taxes go into separate trust funds. A senior is eligible to receive Social Security (is *vested*) when he or she accumulates *40 Social Security credits*, which represent 40 quarters (10 years) of earned income of at least $4,520 per year. Of course, most people work longer than 10 years and earn more than $4,520 per year. This is good, because *Social Security benefits are calculated as a percentage of an average of the highest 35 years of a person's income*.

The Social Security benefits table resembles a reverse version of the graduated income tax table. For example, someone with an earned income of $50,000 and an average employment history who retired in 2012 received an annual benefit of $21,324. If the system were *not* graduated, someone with an $110,000 income would receive 11/5 as much, or $46,913 per year. But that higher earner only received $31,260, the maximum full benefit. This means *the contributions of higher earners (up to $110,000 of their income) partially fund the benefits of lower earners*. Nonetheless, *Social Security is not a government hand-out for anyone*. It is money recipients have earned through years of their payments and those by their employers to the Social Security Trust Fund.

If you are *62 or over*, you may apply for a Social Security pension. *At age 62, you get 75% of your full (age 66) benefit*. And you get roughly ½ a percent of your 62-year-old benefit more for each month you delay before starting, until you reach age 66. If you delay further, you add 2/3 of a percent of your full benefit for each month you wait until 70, at which point *you reach the maximum benefit you could ever receive*. Throughout this process, if you have earned income, you continue to pay payroll taxes on it and may increase the amount of your benefit (if your current earned income is more than any earlier year used in your average). But if you have little or no earned income, *you will receive the amount you receive in the first month of getting Social Security for the rest of your life, with cost-of-living (COLA) adjustments along the way*.

If you receive benefits before age 66, *earned* income above a pre-set amount ($14,200 in 2013) reduces your benefit by $1 for every "extra" $2 you earn. So if you earn $16,200, your benefit is reduced by $1,000. However, there is no limit on rental and investment income, another advantage for those with capital gains income. Then, at age 66, earned income no longer counts against your benefit. So, *people who still have significant earned income may have to wait until 66 to receive Social Security*. You may wait longer, but *nobody, retired or not, should wait past 70.*

The decision of when to take Social Security should be based on a comparison of how much you would receive for the rest of your life with different starting ages. If you start getting benefits at 62, leaving aside any future COLA adjustments (which are always too small to keep up with inflation), it is easy to calculate how much you will receive by any age. The Social Security website or a local office can tell you how much you would get if you wait to any age from 62 to 70, with the estimates based on two scenarios: 1) continuing to work until those ages, possibly building up your 35-year earnings average, or 2) retiring now and waiting to apply for Social Security.

The key number in this decision is the *cross-over age*, the point when two calculations are equal. For example, I began taking Social Security at age 62 years 9 months. If I stopped working then and waited until 66 to apply, I would have received 20.5% more each month for the rest of my life. But I would have given up benefit checks between ages 62 years 9 months and 66. At 79 years 9 months, I would have received the same amount from either decision. So 79 years 9 months was my cross-over age. When I compared starting at 62 years 9 months to starting at the maximum benefit age of 70, my cross-over age was 81 years 4 months. Of course, depending on how long I live, the advantage of waiting could either never happen or give me a little or a lot more life-time income. Moreover, for whatever it is worth, at 63 my life expectancy was 81½, only 1 3/4 years past my cross-over age. However, if you are 66 when you retire and compare that age to 70, the calculation will be slightly different. Past age 66, the larger increments for each additional month lessen the time to your crossover age, making waiting as long as possible more advantageous.

If you find it difficult to decide which option is best for you, talk to an accountant or financial planner about the benefits and costs of beginning Social Security at different ages.

✦

It is essential to estimate how much you will get from Social Security. Without that number, it is impossible to know what you will need from other sources of income. Even though all recent proposals to guarantee full funding for benefits past 2033 have been rejected by one political party or the other, it is foolish to eliminate Social Security from your retirement planning.

Let's begin by estimating Social Security benefits for older middle-class *individuals* who worked at least 35 years and took full retirement benefits in 2012. They earn $20,000 to $31,260 per year from Social Security, depending on their earnings history. However, the average 2011 benefit was only $14,172 due to workers who received low wages throughout their lives, those who receive spousal benefits (see below), and those who took benefits before reaching full-benefit age. *Your* amount will depend on your "best" 35 years as an income earner and the age at which you first receive benefits.

If both spouses qualify for benefits, each receives the Social Security pension they have earned. But if only one spouse has earned a benefit, the other may receive a "*spousal benefit.*" This pays up to half the benefit claimed by the vested spouse. So, if the vested spouse takes an early benefit, both benefits are permanently diminished. This is the best reason for a vested spouse with a non-qualifying spouse to wait as long as possible, up to age 70, before taking Social Security. In any case, *when one spouse dies, the surviving spouse may only receive one benefit,* keeping *the larger of the two received when both were alive (another reason for the higher benefit receiver to wait as long as possible).* This means middle-class *couples* who retired in 2012 and took full benefits receive between $32,000 and $63,000.

Of course, you or your spouse may retire before reaching Social Security age, giving you no or one benefit for a few years before getting two. Meanwhile, the Supreme Court's 2013 ruling that overturned the 1996 Defense of Marriage Act (DOMA) allows married same-sex couples to qualify for the same benefits as other married couples. The situation for same-sex couples who are not married because they live in states that do not allow them to marry is still up in the air.

BENEFITS FOR FUTURE RETIREES

Now let's turn to the more difficult task of predicting Social Security benefits for young Americans. If benefits were based on the 2012 formula, a person retiring in 2052 might receive 3.24 times what a similar earner receives today. That is how much incomes and Social Security taxes will rise if they keep pace with a 3% inflation rate. So a person earning $50,000 today would receive a full benefit of $68,700 in 2052, while a person earning $110,000 today would receive a benefit of $100,600. Of course, these benefits would be paid in deflated 2052 dollars.

Unfortunately, this is unlikely to happen. People in their 20s and 30s who work for 35 years and end up with an income equal to $50,000 in 2012 dollars are more likely to receive a full Social Security benefit of $42,000, while someone with an income equal to $110,000 in 2012 dollars will receive $65,000. This is roughly 65% of what would be received by today's formula, less than the 77% projected by the federal government. However, by then more Social Security income will probably be taxed or go toward Medicare costs. So, a household with two benefits that had a 2012 gross income of $80,000 *is likely to receive an effective Social Security benefit of $75,000 in 2052.*

Given the effect of inflation on salaries over long periods and the uncertainty about future Social Security formulas in relation to today's formula, the above numbers may turn out to be too high or too low. But as you near retirement, you should be able to more accurately project your benefit. If it is higher than expected, adjust your savings goals downward or retire sooner. If it is lower, adjust in the opposite direction.

DEFINED-BENEFIT PENSIONS

A defined-benefit pension gives a retiree a guaranteed annual income. This is what people call "getting a pension." In the past, many private companies had defined-benefit pensions, with the employer contributing to a pension fund, thereby paying some of the employee's earnings without it counting as taxable income. In many cases, the employee also made contributions to the fund, with that income similarly untaxed in that year. In addition, estimates of the employee's federal and state income tax and payroll taxes were withheld and sent directly to the IRS and state tax agency by the employer. So *employees learned to think of their after-pension, after-tax income as their "full" income.*

Pension contributions were placed in a professionally managed *company-held* pension fund. When an employee retired, his or her pension was drawn from this fund. Along with other benefits offered by the company, such as partial payment of health insurance premiums or access to life insurance, the employee received a monthly pension check for the rest of his or her life.

After reaching the number of years needed to qualify for a pension (becoming vested), the amount of the pension was adjusted upward for salary increases and each additional year of employment with the company. At the time of retirement, retirees were usually given two options: take the full pension they had earned and have the pension end when the retiree dies, *or* take a lesser amount, in which case a surviving spouse would continue to get the reduced pension until the end of his or her life. However, if the spouse died first, the retiree was stuck with the lower pension for the rest of his or her life. Some pensions also received cost-of-living allowance (COLA) increases, although few kept up with the full effect of inflation.

This kind of pension is disappearing from the private sector. Instead, many companies now only offer "*defined-contribution*" pension plans (see Chapter 10). Unfortunately, some older workers and retirees who were promised pensions have seen them reduced as a cost cutting measure as their companies ran into financial trouble. Or, if the company went into bankruptcy, it may have gotten permission from a judge as part of a "re-structuring" plan to eliminate pension guarantees entirely. And lastly, if the pension fund was heavily invested in the company's stock, the fund may have lost value as the company descended into financial crisis. In these situations, retirees might also lose company contributions to health insurance or other promised benefits.

At present, *defined-benefit pensions are most common in the public sector* for teachers, firemen, police, civil servants, politicians, and workers in public hospitals, prisons, and courts. But even in this arena, pensions are under attack. Nevertheless, *if you have a defined-benefit pension, calculate how much you will get from it and deduct that amount from the total retirement income you will need.* And remember, if you get a pension, it is not a gift. It is something you have earned by your employer (and perhaps you) paying some of *your* gross income into the fund.

THE FAMILY HOME AND OTHER REAL ESTATE

The hardest asset to evaluate as a source of income is a family home. For me, the solution to this problem is simple. *Count the equity in your home as wealth in your estate; but assume it will generate little or no income in retirement* since you will probably continue to live in your home or spend the proceeds from selling it on your next housing choice.

Thus, unless you get a *reverse mortgage* (see below) the wealth tied up in your home will be a greater benefit to your heirs than to you. However, it is likely *homeownership expenses will decline after you retire*. You may get a break on property taxes and, if you have paid off your mortgage, the lack of mortgage payments should free up money to spend on other budget items.

Lastly, if you own *income-producing properties or a business,* calculate how much *net* income (gross income less all expenses) you will get from them after retirement. As with Social Security and defined-benefit pensions, subtract this amount from the total income you will need. Or you could sell investment properties or your business and add the proceeds to your savings, an easier thing for most people to do than selling their own home. In either case, be conservative in estimating the worth of properties or businesses. Recent history has demonstrated how easily we all can over-value them.

BORROWING ON YOUR OWN ASSETS TO GET INCOME

There are two ways other than taking distributions from savings by which you can use your assets to generate income.

First, in a program established by Congress and President Ronald Reagan in 1988, financial companies offer *reverse mortgages*, which are insured by the federal government and sold to elderly people who have a lot of equity in their homes but too little income. Purchasers of reverse mortgages remain the owner of their homes and are still responsible for repairs, home insurance, and taxes. But they sell some or all of the equity in the home to the financial company. In return, they receive a *tax-free* monthly check for as long as they live. They also retain the right to live in their home for as long as they like or until they die. In traditional reverse mortgages, when the homeowner leaves the home the financial company keeps the equity sold to it. In many cases, this means it can sell the home.

However, some reverse mortgages now allow the homeowner (or heirs) to buy back the equity that was sold to the financial company.

Reverse mortgages are the only way to turn home equity into income without having to pay back the money received. Financial companies base the decision of how much to pay the homeowner on a monthly basis on the market value of the home; their estimate of its future value; the return they expect to make when the home is sold; and actuarial tables that predict how long the homeowner will live, which tells them how long they will have to pay him or her. To make a profit on this arrangement, they give themselves a healthy margin of error in these calculations. In most cases, heirs also lose out on that part of the value of the home. So, if you have a lot of equity in your home and need more income, it is far better to sell your house, however difficult that may be, and rent a more modest place to live, with the proceeds going into savings. With this strategy, you will have more income and the value of your home, now in investments, will stay in your estate.

Second, people who are worried about getting enough return on their savings may purchase *an annuity* from a financial or insurance company. This can be done with some or all of their savings. The financial company invests the money "sold" to them, keeping the interest, dividends, and growth in value it earns, while absorbing any losses. In return, the annuity owner gets a tax-free income for as long as he or she lives. This has the advantage of turning part of your wealth into a knowable amount of income. That being said, annuities now come in many varieties. You can buy an annuity with one large payment or smaller payments over several years. An annuity may pay a fixed income or one that increases (is indexed) over time. However, an annuity owner must buy an indexed annuity at least 10 years before receiving income from it. This allows the financial company to make money on the homeowner's money before issuing checks. Currently, indexed annuities may only be sold to people over age 45. Thus, an annuity holder may begin getting checks in his or her mid-50s at the earliest, although many annuity owners wait until they retire.

As with reverse mortgages, some annuities allow the annuity holder to buy back principal from the financial company. Others allow payments to be delayed to as late as age 80 with the eventual income increasing while they wait, mirroring the buildup of cash value in a whole life insurance policy. Some annuities have no up-front fees, while others charge high fees when they are bought. And some retirement investment accounts can be "rolled over" into an annuity after retirement, a strategy that may lower taxes on income in later years. Lastly, some annuities include a death benefit. However, heirs may have to pay tax on money they receive from these annuities. So, before purchasing an annuity, consult an accountant about the tax implications of the one you are considering.

Financial companies sell annuities because they are confident they will make money on them. With or without up-front fees, they all charge for handling the money, issuing checks, the buying back of principal, or issuing a death benefit. So they always end up with some of the annuity holder's money. Moreover, I do not believe the future is so bleak it makes sense to buy an annuity as a long-term "defensive" investment tactic. Neither, obviously, do the companies that sell annuities. However, if *you* believe stock markets will collapse or your principal will shrink so much you won't get enough income from your savings, it might be worth considering an annuity in order to eliminate the risk of your making bad investment decisions.

BUSINESS AND WORK INCOME

Those with income from a business or who plan to work in retirement should calculate how much they will earn from these endeavors after retirement. But remember, if you retire before Social Security's full benefit age, earned income may count against the benefit you would otherwise get, making it necessary to wait to receive Social

Security. As important, be conservative when estimating how much you will earn from a business or how long you will be able to work. After all, as you age, health problems or other difficulties may make it impossible to earn this money.

✦

In summary, once you know how much you will get from non-savings sources of income, don't panic about the amount you have to save in order to retire with an adequate income. *Panic just serves as an excuse for not saving*. Remember that "life is long" and you may end up with other sources of retirement income. In any case, if you start saving now one thing is certain: you will end up better off than if you don't save.

Or, as the Nike ads say, "Just do it."

CHAPTER 10

SAVING FOR RETIREMENT, THE KEY TO WEALTH

Questions: What is the difference between a pension and a 401(k)? How about IRAs? Why do I have to contribute to my retirement savings when others don't need to do it? What should I count as retirement savings?

ONCE YOU KNOW YOUR TARGET INCOME FOR YEAR-1 OF RETIREMENT and how much income will come from other sources, you are ready to calculate the savings you will need.

While a lucky few receive inheritances or gifts, for most people *saved money* is in four forms:

- *retirement savings plans at work*
- *individual retirement accounts "at home"*
- *non-retirement (brokerage) investment accounts*
- *certificates of deposit, money market funds and bank accounts (altogether, cash)*

SAVING AT WORK: DEFINED-CONTRIBUTION PLANS

Let's begin with *401(k) Plans.* An employee cannot set up a 401(k)

Plan. It must be *offered by an employer* as a way for employees to save for retirement. Contributions to a 401(k) and growth within it are not taxed as income. However, when a person withdraws money from these accounts (takes distributions), that money is taxed as income in that year. If distributions are taken before age 59½, there is also a 10% penalty. And distributions *must* be taken from a 401(k) after age 70½.

The investment choices in 401(k) Plans are limited. Investments must be selected from a list of mutual funds, stocks, and bonds offered by a financial company the employer has authorized to manage the Plan. Since high management fees and poor investment decisions, unfortunately common problems with 401(k)s, may severely reduce the growth of your money, if your employer offers several Plans, research each one's level of risk, performance history (growth *after* fees are taken), and portfolio. Then select the one that fits your goals and comfort level. Lastly, owning stock in the company you work for in a 401(k) *and* earning a living from it at the same time is the opposite of being diversified. Avoiding this mistake also preserves the biggest advantage of *a 401(k) Plan*: unlike a pension, it *is in your name*. So your savings should not be at risk if your company declines or goes out of business.

If your 401(k) Plan does not keep up with major stock markets over a significant period of time, move your money to one offered by your employer that is doing better. But don't make changes often. Remember, *when it comes to retirement savings, only long-term results matter.* And, if you change jobs, take your 401(k) with you. Any 401(k) may be *"rolled over"* into another 401(k) or at certain times into an IRA (see below) or annuity with no loss of value in the Plan. However, *if a roll-over is done incorrectly, the IRS will treat the entire amount as having passed through your hands, taxing all of it as income in the year of the transfer*. This must be avoided at all costs. So consult an accountant or your new employer's 401(k) fund manager before doing anything.

For modest-income earners, money put into a 401(k) is deducted from their adjusted gross income. So, in the 15% tax bracket, the federal government reduces the tax that must be paid by $15 for every $100 contributed, up to the allowed limits for that taxpayer. Since the employee would have spent that $15 on taxes anyway, an "out-of-pocket" contribution of $85 makes a $15 return (17.7%) on the day it is contributed.

Employers may also match some employee contributions. This makes the start-up return on out-of-pocket money even greater. Let's look at two common schemes. First, if a company matches ¼ of contributions up to $4,000, making a $4,000 contribution triggers a $600 tax saving and $1,000 in matching funds from the employer. So, an "out-of-pocket" contribution of $3,400 turns into $5,000, thereby earning *47%* before it is even invested. Or second, if an employee earns $40,000, is in the 15% tax bracket, and the company matches contributions up to 5% of the employee's pay, contributing $2,000 to a 401(k) triggers an employer contribution of $2,000 and a $300 tax saving. So $1,700 out-of-pocket becomes $4,000, for an instant *135% return*. In both cases, contributions are allowed to grow over the following years with no tax paid until distributions are taken. The lesson in this is simple. *If your company offers a 401(k), contribute to it. If it offers a matching program, make at least the level of contribution that triggers the maximum matching amount.* Failing to do so is leaving free government *and* company money "on the table."

DEFERRED-COMPENSATION PLANS

Employers may require or allow you to delay some income until later. These are called *"deferred compensation"* benefits. For example, an employee may be given a raise that will not be paid until retirement or stock options that may be exercised at a later date. When these benefits are actually received, the money is put into a *457 Plan*,

403B Plan, or 402(b) Plan depending on the position of the employee and the kind of company or organization for which the employee works. With the employee's consent, the employer may also put up to 25% of the employee's pay, with a maximum of $50,000 per year and other limits tied to the employee's adjusted gross income, into a *Simplified Employee Pension Plan (SEP-IRA)*. While the employee must establish the SEP-IRA, the employer makes the contribution to it. None of the money in these plans is treated as taxable income until the plan holder takes distributions from them. With the exception of a 457 Plan, there is also a 10% penalty for taking a distribution before age 59½. But in all these plans, *you must start taking distributions at 70½*. Lastly, if you improperly roll over any of these plans, the whole amount is taxed in that year.

In a related mechanism, *an employer may offer a monetary incentive to get an employee to retire immediately*. After all, a replacement employee usually earns less than a "seasoned" employee, while the cost of benefits may also be reduced. So, even after paying the incentive, labor costs may be lowered for years to come. This technique is also used when lay-offs are imminent. If older workers take the incentive, a workforce can be trimmed without firing anyone. Retirement incentive money is put into a 457, 403B, or 402(b) when you retire, and is not counted as taxable income until distributions are taken. Some retirement incentives also "sweeten the pot" in a second way. For those who will receive a pension, employers may offer to add extra years of credit to the employee's record. This increases the pension for the rest of the employee's life. There is no more powerful incentive than this when it comes to retirement timing.

Lastly, some employers offer older employees *lump sum buy-out packages*. To avoid a heavy tax bill at the moment of retirement, these can be converted into an annuity or IRA. Once the lump-sum is accepted, the retiree gets no further pension, although he or she may still get other benefits like access to company-sponsored health and life insurance.

If you have money in a 401(k), 457, 402b, 403B, or SEP-IRA, these amounts should be counted as savings. You should also be prepared to manage these accounts and consider whether to transfer some of them to other retirement accounts once you are allowed to do so. An accountant or financial planner can help you with these decisions.

INDIVIDUAL "REGISTERED" RETIREMENT ACCOUNTS

In addition to saving for retirement at work, you can do it "at home" by putting money into *Individual Retirement Accounts (IRAs)*. There are several types of IRAs, but all are "registered" with the IRS in order to qualify for special tax treatment. The limits listed below were for 2012.

Within limits set in relation to adjusted gross income the maximum contribution to a *regular IRA* is $5,000 per year or $6,000 for anyone over 50. This allows older savers to "catch up" a little if they are behind in their savings plan. As with a 401(k), the federal government does not tax contributions or growth in an IRA over the years. But all distributions are taxed in the year they are taken and there is a 10% penalty for withdrawals before age 59½ unless the money is used for approved education costs. In addition, *once you reach 70½, you are no longer allowed to make contributions to regular IRAs and must take distributions from them.*

People who are self-employed may also contribute to a *SEP-IRA*. In this case, the person is both the employee who creates the plan and the employer who makes contributions to it. The limits are the same as for any other employer. Those who have a SEP-IRA and a regular IRA may contribute to both, although the amounts escaping immediate taxation in each may be reduced. Nevertheless, the tax benefit of contributing to a SEP-IRA helps make up for the employer contributions self-employed people have to make to payroll taxes.

Finally, those with *earned* incomes may contribute to a *Roth-IRA* whether they contribute to a regular IRA or SEP-IRA or not. Roth contributions are limited to $5,000 or $6,000 if you are 50 or older. But unlike other IRAs, there is *no age limit for making contributions or having to take distributions*. So a Roth can be preserved and grow until the end of life. More important, there is no tax on growth within a Roth-IRA or on distributions taken after age 59½. So income tax is paid "up front" to avoid tax at "the back end." However, there are income limits for contributing to a Roth-IRA. In 2012, individuals who earned over $110,000 were only allowed to contribute a portion of the above-listed amounts, while those earning over $125,000 couldn't contribute to a Roth-IRA at all. For joint filers, the comparable "ceiling" amounts were $173,000 and $183,000.

If you can afford to contribute to a Roth-IRA and are eligible to do so, this is the best savings option of all. No other retirement account allows you to keep savings intact past 70½ or avoid taxation on growth in your account for the rest of your life. And this can add up to a lot of money. To refer back to the compound interest chart in Chapter 4, if you contribute $1,000 to a regular IRA and are in the 15% tax bracket, you get a $150 tax deduction (or, starting in 2014, a tax credit). If you get a 7% return over the next 40 years, your $1,000 grows to $14,963. But when you take distributions you pay tax on that entire amount. By comparison, if you contribute $1,000 to a Roth-IRA, you lose the initial $150 deduction. But when you later take distributions you don't have to pay tax at all, even on the growth that occurred within the Roth over the years. So you have $13,963 ($14,963 – the initial $1,000) that is not taxed at all as long as you live.

Unfortunately, most Americans find it hard to contribute to a Roth-IRA because this would require them to pay tax on money they cannot touch for years. Thus, examples in this and later chapters assume "at home" savings will be in tax-deferred accounts. Given the unique advantages of a Roth, however, it makes sense to roll over some retirement money into a Roth when you retire, paying the taxes at that point to get tax-free growth and income in following years, with the added benefit of preserving some of your savings past age 70½. An accountant can help you decide if this strategy is right for you.

All IRA Plans are flexible. You may pick assets from an almost limitless menu of investments that match your specifications for diversification, risk, or changing goals you may have at different times. Nor do you have to be an expert stock picker to take advantage of IRAs. You can hire an investment advisor to do this job for you or limit your holdings to mutual funds that hold many different stocks and bonds. This also makes it easier to stay diversified.

NON-REGISTERED SAVINGS

It is important to *save for emergencies and education costs that will come up before retirement.* These funds can be kept in bank accounts, money market funds, certificates of deposit, or be put into non-registered ("brokerage") investment accounts that may hold cash, stocks, bonds, and mutual funds. "Rainy day" funds should total at least 4 months of living expenses and be invested in a way that allows you to quickly turn it into cash. This is what financial professionals call *liquidity*. There may also be situations in which you can save more than you are allowed to put into registered retirement accounts, as when you sell a house or receive "extra" income, a bonus that cannot be deferred, a gift, or an inheritance. In these cases, excess savings should be put into non-registered accounts and then invested with a less liquid (more long-term) profile.

With the exception of insurance, gift, and inheritance proceeds, *money put into non-registered savings is taxed as income* in the year of the deposit. *Interest, dividends, and the sale of assets within* the account (realized gain) *are also taxed immediately,* whether you use that money that year or not. But if you sell an asset and take a loss, you may deduct the loss from that year's income. Lastly, *when you withdraw money you pay no penalty no matter your age and only realized gain that has not already been taxed counts as income*. There are also no age limits for making deposits into or being forced to take withdrawals from non-registered savings, although when you retire it may make sense to roll some of these funds over into a Roth-IRA to avoid tax on future growth.

The main purpose of non-registered savings for modest income earners is to avoid tapping retirement savings prematurely and paying a penalty to do so. But non-registered savings accounts may go unused or grow. So, estimate how much will be in these accounts when you retire and *count them as savings*.

SUMMARY: THE "SAVING HABIT" OR THE TORTOISE WINS THE RACE

Many people intend to save. They set up 401(k) Plans, IRAs, 529 Educational Savings Plans, and non-registered investment and savings accounts. But few contribute to these accounts consistently. The reason is simple. Most people don't have a budget and keep spending until they run out of money each month. And those *with* a budget list all expenditures, including daily costs *and* the amount they intend to save. When needs exceed expectations, a circumstance that happens often to most of us, the thing that gets cut out of the budget is saving. Moreover, *there is always an "emergency" that uses up extra income*. There are appliances to buy, home repairs, car problems, programs for children, holiday gifts, unexpected medical or dental bills, and vacations. Who would argue any of these were wasteful spending? But with great sympathy for this dilemma, *if you don't save consistently, you will not have enough money for future emergencies or retirement*.

The solution to this dilemma is simple. *Create a yearly budget and honor it. Within that budget, pay your savings first.* This is what accountants call "paying yourself first." *Then pay your taxes.* Lastly, *budget the rest of your income for your other needs.* This is why having a 401(k) or other savings plan at work is so helpful. This lowers your tax bill and gets you into the habit of treating after-savings after-tax income as your entire income. If you can do the same with IRAs and non-registered savings, it will be even better. But if you don't develop this habit, it is all but certain you will not make contributions to your retirement savings consistently. And if that happens, no investment strategy will create the wealth you will need in your later years.

PART 2

SAVING FOR LIFE

CHAPTER 11

MODEL PLANS, REAL POSSIBILITIES

Part 1: Plans for the Older Set

Questions: How much wealth should I have by the time I retire? How do I figure out my "magic savings number," like the ones I hear about on television? Will I ever be able to retire?

WHEN YOU BEGIN SAVING FOR RETIREMENT, IT IS HARD TO KNOW HOW big a "nest egg" you will eventually need or how much to save each year to create it. Luckily, we have already dealt with the elements that go into these calculations. Our goal in this chapter is to put them together to create successful models for older adults. In the next chapter, we will create similar models for young adults.

PLANNING YOUR PLAN: PROJECTIONS AND ADJUSTMENTS

There are *six steps* to constructing a successful retirement savings plan.

- Figure out how much income you will need in the first year of retirement. This calculation depends on your current level of income and your estimate for inflation in the intervening years.

- Add up the retirement income that will come from Social Security and other non-savings sources. Subtract this amount from the total in Step 1. The rest will have to come from the return on your savings.

- Estimate the return you expect to make on your savings *before* retirement.

- Estimate the return you expect to make on your saved money *after* retirement.

- Use the above calculations to estimate how much savings you will need when you retire.

- Determine the amount you should save each year to reach your savings goal by the year of your retirement.

The following discussion will make it easier to see the connections among these steps. We have already dealt with Step 1 in earlier chapters by estimating the inflation rate over the next 40 years at 3% per year and calculating the income needed in year-1 of retirement as 77% of the final pre-retirement income for most modest-income households. The calculation in Step 2 will be unique to you. So let's begin with Step 3, estimating the return received before retirement.

The performance of the stock markets largely determines how your investments do. If the markets do well, your savings are likely to grow faster than expected. If this happens early in your adulthood, the positive effect can last for years. But if the markets do poorly, you will have to increase your contributions to retirement accounts, delay retirement, or plan on living on less when you do so. The key is to *stay flexible and adjust if you must.* Just remember, if your investments do well in a boom (*bull*) market, this does not prove you are an investment genius. And if they do badly in a down (*bear*) market, it does not mean you are an investment idiot. Your success as an investor is partly based on skill, patience, sound judgment, and good advice; but it is also affected by luck and accidental timing. So stay humble in good times and confident in bad times.

While this may sound obvious, to adjust your plan along the way you must first know how you are doing. That is why *I checked our plan's progress once a year*, writing a summary of our current income and net worth (assets minus debts) and my projection of where we might be in 5 years, 10 years, and when I reached age 65. This let us know if we needed to make immediate changes to our spending or savings habits. I also read current economic opinions to help me decide if we should revise my projections of how our income and savings might grow over the years *before* retirement, and whether my estimate of our return on savings *after* retirement was still reasonable. By 1994, I was also estimating our Social Security benefits and my teacher's pension.

Lastly, *I reviewed the performance of our investments every six months*, while encouraging our stockbroker to call us whenever he or she felt we needed to make changes in our portfolio. In order to simplify our investment choices and remain diversified, we limited our holdings to *closed-end* (CEF), *exchange-traded* (ETF), and *traditional mutual funds*. Some funds hold real estate while others hold stocks of mid- to large-sized American companies, world-wide stocks, and/or corporate and government bonds. We also held onto our investments in Canada. This strategy made us less dependent on the performance of individual companies, one sector of the economy, or even the American economy as a whole.

Once this routine was established, we did *not* check our plan's progress at other times of the year. The last thing we wanted was to make investment strategy or retirement planning central to our lives on a daily, weekly, or even monthly basis. Nor did we want to change investments whenever there were short-term swings in the stock markets. This is one area of life where too much worry or "instant" information can lead to mistakes. However, my reviews assured us our plan and investments were not going in the wrong direction on "automatic pilot."

Once completed, I kept my reviews in a file at home (first on paper in a file cabinet and later on a computer). Part of the fun of doing this was I could look back later and see how well I had done predicting our plan's progress. But there was also a serious purpose to this routine. By simultaneously looking at our past, present, and future, the accuracy of my analysis, benchmarks, and long-term projections slowly improved.

Interestingly, Vanguard Funds, the second largest American 401(k) management company and a major mutual fund provider, issued new *retirement savings benchmarks* in 2013. According to Vanguard, people should have savings equal to four times their gross income at age 40, six times their income at 50, and *eight times their income at 67*, the age Vanguard targets for retirement. This is a remarkably simple approach to benchmarking. However, it is unclear what estimates Vanguard used for future inflation, income growth, or post-retirement return on savings. Moreover, this "one-size-fits-all" guideline does not appear to take into account the variability of people's non-savings sources of income.

For many people, paying a financial planner or a company like Vanguard (there are many others) to develop a retirement plan is a necessity. If you go that route, make sure your plan has *benchmarks that tell you if you are falling behind, on target, or ahead of your plan's projections*. And check these benchmarks at least yearly. After all, no matter how good your financial advisor is you still have to evaluate his or her advice, monitor your progress, and make adjustments when necessary. That being said, it is a central theme of this book that *you can do this job for yourself*. So let's get started.

A SAVINGS PLAN FOR THE "OLDER SET"

Let's begin with a savings plan for a 62-year-old couple retiring in 2013 with a final pre-retirement gross income of $80,000, the mid-point of modest-income households as defined in Chapter 2.

INCOME NEEDED FROM SAVINGS

To maintain their lifestyle, our couple will need a year-1 retirement income of $61,600. If only one spouse worked, that individual's *full* Social Security benefit plus a spousal benefit would *total $37,500*. However, since our couple is taking benefits at age 62, they will receive *75% of their full benefits, or $28,125*. Our couple might have other combinations of incomes totaling $80,000 that would give them slightly higher Social Security benefits, but to be conservative we will use $28,125 as the age 62 Social Security benefit in the following charts. This is 35.1% of our couple's final pre-retirement income, less than the average of 40% for current recipients. Given these figures, *our couple's non-Social Security income need will be $61,600–$28,125, or $33,475*.

If either spouse has a defined-benefit pension, business, part-time job, investment property, left over non-registered savings or has received an inheritance, the income from these sources should be subtracted from $33,475. This would lower the amount of savings needed. However, if either of our couple has significant post-retirement *earned* income, that person might have to wait until 66 to get Social Security.

The above calculations illustrate why it is often better to wait beyond age 62 to retire. *If our couple were turning 66* in 2013, they would get \$37,500 from Social Security. So *they would only need \$24,150 from other sources*. Or, if they waited to retire at age 64, they would receive 87.5% of their full Social Security benefit. They would also have two more years to make contributions to and put off taking distributions from their investment accounts. While they would need slightly more income in year-1 of retirement because of inflation in the two extra years before retiring, they would have more savings, perhaps larger Social Security benefits, and in all probability two fewer years of retirement. In short, they would be in a much better situation.

THE NECESSARY LEVEL OF SAVINGS, AND HOW TO GET THERE

Let's look at the *worst case scenario* for our 62-year old couple. If the only sources of income are Social Security and savings, savings would have to generate a year-1 retirement income of \$33,475. *With a post-retirement return of 5% per year and a goal of not using up saved money, this would require savings of \$669,500. If we project a 4.5% return, our couple would need \$743,890.* These totals represent 8.37 and 9.3 times our couple's final pre-retirement income, more demanding numbers than the 8.0 multiple (\$640,000) suggested by Vanguard Funds.

Let's take a closer look at post-retirement returns on savings. Retirement planners often advise people use "*the 4% rule,*" which posits a household should take distributions equal to 4% of its savings in year-1 of retirement. If their return is more than 4%, they take a higher percentage the *next* year. If their return is less, they take a lower percentage. Then they adjust future distributions based on how their money did in each previous year, staying even with or ahead of how much savings they need so their money will last at least until the end of their lives.

The 4% rule makes a lot of sense because it keeps people from overspending early in retirement. It does not, however, predict what *your* return will be over many years after taking 4% in year-1 of retirement. And this is a number you or a retirement planner must estimate to construct a savings plan, long before you retire. There are many opinions about this number. Many financial planners project that with a very low-risk post-retirement investment strategy, if people take distributions that average 4% through good times and bad their savings will last until the end of life. However, other experts think retirees with moderate growth investment strategies that are still safe should be able to average 5% distributions. Meanwhile, the Social Security Administration projects an annual return of *5.7%* on the Social Security Trust Fund through 2033, while the New York State Teachers' Retirement Fund projects an annual return of *8%* over the next decade.

To be conservative, we will only look at returns of 4.5% and 5%. But if we added a column for a still reasonable 5.5% return to Charts 11-1A and 11-1B, it would show a picture in which our couple could retire sooner, set a lower savings goal ($602,550), or draw more income from savings in retirement. Moreover, these numbers are based on our couple *not* using up any of their savings until they are forced to do so by the rules governing tax-deferred accounts. Interestingly, if we project a return of 5.2% and keep the goal of preserving savings, we would get Vanguard's savings goal of $640,000. Perhaps this is what they did to set their savings benchmark.

✦

Next, let's turn to Step 4: estimating how much our couple should have saved annually to arrive at their target savings number. Once again, let's start by looking at recent history. While it is often lamented that *individual* incomes have not kept up with inflation over the last 20 years and inflation-adjusted *household* incomes have fallen in the last 10, increases in incomes for *all* Americans have outpaced inflation by 17.9% in the last 30 years. And middle-class households have done better than the national average. As a result, *middle-class household incomes are much higher today than they were in 1970, even in 1970 dollars.*

Despite the great variability in the income history of different households, to create the models represented in Charts 11-1A and 11-1B, we have to imagine a pattern for the income growth of our couple. We will use a steady growth from $18,000 in 1972 to $80,000 in 2012. This is slightly less than 4% per year. If you are 62 years old, of course, *your* income growth over the last 40 years has depended on factors unique to you, such as your career choices, health history, and, for women, perhaps childbearing and child-raising history. However, to again use New York State teachers as an example, in 1968 a first-year teacher earned $7,000, while in 2008 a new teacher earned $28,000 to $40,000, depending on the school district. This is a four- to six-fold increase in salary. More to the point, a teacher who was hired in 1968 no longer earns a starting salary. By 2009, a New York State teacher with 30-40 years of experience earned $60,000 to $90,000, while some in New York City and its suburbs earned well over $100,000. As unthinkable as those numbers would have seemed in 1968 (or $7,000 seems to teachers today), the income of a teacher with 40 years of experience has increased 9- to 14-fold over a period in which inflation has eroded the value of the dollar to about one-third of its 1968 worth.

When we consider both effects together, a New York State teacher's inflation-adjusted income has tripled or quadrupled in 40 years. In discussions with friends my age who are in other fields of employment, the pattern is similar. As a result of raises, promotions, and job changes, most say their incomes have grown far more than inflation has eroded the dollars they spent or saved.

Since most people save a set percentage of their income each year, this robust income growth has made it easier for baby-boomers to accumulate retirement savings. *Here's a three-step plan our 62-year-old couple could have used. In the first 7 years of saving, 1% of gross income could have gone to a rainy-day fund, 1.5% to education savings, and 6% to retirement savings, for a total savings rate of 8.5%. In the next 18 years, 1.5% could have gone to education and 7% to retirement. Then, in the final 15 years before retirement, 8.5% could have gone to retirement. Assuming that immediate tax savings were important throughout this process, as much as allowed should have been put into 401(k)s, IRAs, or other tax-deferred investment accounts.*

In contrast to this recommendation, many financial planners suggest an annual saving rate of 10% or more. While this would make it far easier to reach long-term savings targets, modest-income families would struggle to meet this savings rate when dealing with their own student loans, starting a family, buying a home, facing medical issues, or paying for children's college educations. Since these "special" times make up a large part of adulthood, it is more likely modest-income families would be able to sustain an 8.5% annual savings rate. Nevertheless, it is important to remember that it does not matter what savings rate a couple sets unless both spouses commit to the idea of treating savings, including money in rainy-day accounts, as "belonging to the future" and not their present lifestyle. While it might sound harsh, without a life-long honoring of this mutual commitment, even the best wealth-generating plan or investment strategy is doomed to failure.

Aside from meeting their retirement goals, the above *three-step plan* would have funded a full emergency fund in 7 years and sizable 529 Education Savings Plans in 25 years. While those 529 Plans would not have been large enough to pay all college costs, they would have made the costs more manageable during the college years and limited student loan repayments after graduation. *As an added benefit, the federal government would have reduced our couple's income taxes every year, contributing 15% of the money saved for retirement.* Lastly, our couple might have received retirement plan contributions from employers and state tax savings for 529 Plan contributions.

Chart 11-1A illustrates the wealth and retirement income

generated by the above 8.5% savings plan over 30 and 40 years for a couple that had a 2012 income of $80,000, averaged a 7% return during the pre-retirement years, has no left over non-registered savings or other income-generating assets, receive Social Security, and get a 4.5% return on saved money after retirement. Chart 11-1B does the same if our couple gets a 5% return after retirement and all other factors remain the same.

CHART 11-1A: PLAN FOR RETIRING NOW OR IN THE NEAR FUTURE WITH A RETURN OF 4.5% IN RETIREMENT

Retirement Age and Savings Period	2013: age 62/ after 30 years of saving	2013: age 62/ after 40 years of saving	2015: age 64/ after 42 years of saving	2017: age 66/ after 44 years of saving
Income needed	**$61,600**	**$61,600**	**$65,360***	**$69,500***
Social Security	$28,125	$28,125	$32,810*	$37,500*
Other Sources of Income	$0	$0	$0	$0
Income needed from savings	$33,475	$33,475	$32,550	$32,000
Retirement Savings rate/year	6% then 7% then 8.5%	6% then 7% then 8.5%	6% then 7% then 8.5%	6% then 7% then 8.5%
Total Retirement savings	$432,000	$840,000	$920,000*	$1,055,000*
Income from 4.5% return on savings	$19,440	$37,850	$41,400	$47,520
Total income	*$47,565*	***$65,975***	***$74,210***	***$85,020***
Income excess/ shortfall	*-$14,035*	***+$4.375****	***+$8,850****	***+$15,520****

***Note**: If you wait to retire, your first-year income requirement increases because of inflation in the intervening years. But so does your Social Security benefit(s) and total savings.
****Note**: In several columns, our couple has enough income for a secure retirement.

CHART 11-1B: PLAN FOR RETIRING NOW OR IN THE NEAR FUTURE WITH A RETURN OF 5% IN RETIREMENT

Retirement Age and savings period	2013: age 62/ after 30 years of saving	2013: age 62/ after 40 years of saving	2015: age 64/ after 42 years of saving	2017: age 66/ after 44 years of saving
Income needed	**$61,600**	**$61,600**	**$65,360***	**$69,500***
Social Security	$28,125	$28,125	$32,810*	$37,500*
Other Sources of Income	$0	$0	$0	$0
Income needed from savings	$33,475	$33,475	$32,550	$32,000
Retirement savings rate per year	6% then 7% then 8,5%	6% then 7% then 8.5%	6% then 7% then 8.5%	6% then 7% then 8.5%
Total Retirement savings	$432,000	$840,000	$920,000*	$1,055,000*
Income from savings at 5% return	$21,600	$42,900	$46,000	$52,750
Total income	**$49,725**	**$71,025**	**$78,810**	**$90,250**
Income excess/ shortfall	-$11,875	**+$9,425****	**+$13,450****	**+$20,750****

***Note**: If you wait to retire, your first-year income requirement increases because of inflation in the intervening years. But so does your Social Security benefit(s) and total savings.
****Note**: In several columns, our couple has enough income for a secure retirement.

One thing is clear from both charts. *After 30 years of saving, our couple would be short of their income goal.* So, our couple should not retire until they save for a few more years. However, *if our couple saved for 40 years, they should have enough income in retirement, even if they take early Social Security benefits.* Of course, both charts represent the "worst case scenario" in which Social Security and savings are the *only* sources of income and the post-retirement return on savings is 5% or less. In other words, our couple's situation might be much better than shown in Charts 11-1A and 11-1B. This is why so many baby boomers, at least in comparison to earlier American generations, are in a position to enjoy a secure retirement and help their children and grandchildren along the way.

CHAPTER 12

MODEL PLANS, REAL POSSIBILITIES

Part 2: Plans for the Younger Set

LET'S TURN TO A MARRIED COUPLE IN THEIR LATE-20S OR 30S WITH A household income of $80,000 in 2012. They should follow the three-step plan suggested in the last chapter, *starting to save 8.5% of their gross income immediately, or as soon as possible*. Unmarried people should do the same. If there are no children, there is no need to save for children's educations and no way to start a 529 Plan without a named recipient of the funds. So, more money should go into an emergency fund and retirement accounts, making it possible for those who start a family later to retire as early as our model couple. Since a new U.S. Department of Agriculture study predicts it will take the average American family $241,000 to raise a child born in 2012 until age 17 (before college!), those who never have children should find it much easier to save.

Assuming income tax rates remain somewhat similar to today's, the tax savings for a young couple following the 8.5% saving plan will increase as the retirement part of their savings plan increases. So *their "out of pocket" savings rate for all three funds will drop in steps from 7.6% to 7.3% of gross income*. As with our older couple, they might also receive matching funds from an employer for 401(k) contributions and state tax deductions for 529 Plan contributions. This would make the out-of-pocket savings rate lower, even with the same total savings per year.

Young adults should write individual Wills and buy term life insurance as soon as possible. Without a Will, the government might tax away a sizeable part of an estate, while family members might make competing claims on the deceased's assets or children, setting off unwanted legal battles or family feuds. Without life insurance, the death of one adult in the family might derail any wealth-building plan and throw surviving family members into poverty.

✦

Before proceeding, let's pause to look at our savings plan from another perspective. Despite the burden of saving 8.5% each year, this plan should not force those with modest incomes to live without some indulgences. Once you have the habit of paying all your bills within the limits of your after-savings after-tax income and avoiding excess debt (altogether, *living within your means*), spend your remaining income however you want. Go on a vacation. Buy a nicer car. Spend money on your children, a home, restaurant meals, museums, theater, concerts, pro or college sports tickets, a health club, golf, or tennis. Just be sure to save responsibly and stay out of debt *before* indulging yourself in any of these ways.

Despite this advice, it is important to resist the constant encouragements to spend your way to a "better" life and greater debt. Some of it may even seem pleasant. For example, many stores send "personal" thank you notes addressed to customers on a first-name basis, signed by an executive using his or her first name (in reality, mechanically produced). Often these notes come with coupons or "private" sale offers. Other stores send birthday cards, also with special offers, while still others send Happy New Year e-mails that include a heart-felt video message from the CEO thanking you for your business in a way that suggests he or she is your friend. Lastly, you can "friend" any company or store on Facebook or connect with it through other social networking sites. This too comes with "special" discount offers and "warm" interactions.

In another tactic, two companies "cross promote" their products, on the apparent assumption that if you buy one you are a candidate to buy the other, no matter how unrelated the two might be. For example, in 2012 my wife bought a Dole banana at a supermarket with a sticker on it that encouraged her to see the latest animated chipmunk movie. While we didn't see this movie, I am sure Dole bananas and logos were featured in several scenes. Similarly, BMW ran ads featuring their cars' "role" in a Mission Impossible movie we did see. In return, the movie showed the BMW name-plate on the hero's cars in several chase scenes. This kind of "product placement" is everywhere, and it is advertising.

Before laughing at these attempts to promote customer loyalty based on an emotional relationship with a store or product, or trying to get someone to buy something as expensive as a BMW because it is in a "cool" movie, remember that companies do this kind of advertising for a reason. It works. While this would have seemed strange to our grandparents, Americans today apparently want to feel they belong to a consumer "in-group" with elite tastes and buying relationships. Unfortunately, if you are taken in by these manipulations too often, you are likely to spend more than you should and eventually more than you can handle, which will land you in debt. Put simply, *save your affection for people and pets, not stores, companies, or products.*

✦

When we looked at examples for a 62-year-old couple, we saw that with reasonable income growth and saving over the years they could have created the wealth needed for retirement. In several cases, all they have to worry about now is keeping up with inflation *after* retirement and handling mandatory distributions and perhaps higher income taxes after age 70½. But things are different for young Americans. First, they will undoubtedly get a lower percentage of retirement income from Social Security. Second, while inflation will probably continue to deflate the value of the dollar *and* increase incomes, it is not certain incomes will grow as fast *in relation to inflation* as they have over the last 40 years. Not surprisingly, there are many opinions about future income growth and inflation in America, including the warnings of extreme hyperinflation and income stagnation (together, "stagflation") that dominate many financial television and radio shows. However, I believe it is reasonable to assume incomes will at least keep up with inflation over the next 40 years and more likely grow slightly more than inflation.

Chart 12-1 compares three scenarios: annual income growth of 0%, 3% (matching inflation), and 4%, all with a pre-retirement return on savings of 7% and a post-retirement return of 5%. Let's begin with the numbers that will go on this chart.

SOCIAL SECURITY

We have already estimated that if inflation averages 3% per year, a household currently earning $80,000 will draw $75,000 as a full Social Security benefit in 2052, an amount that accounts for likely reductions due to shortfalls in the Social Security Trust Fund, increased taxes on benefits, and higher deductions to cover Medicare. Moreover, since our young couple will need $199,600 to equal a 2012 income of $61,600, Social Security will only contribute 31% of our couple's post-retirement income, far lower than the current average of 40% or the 35% of our model older couple in the last chapter.

INCOME GROWTH AND SAVINGS RATES

If Social Security benefits and savings are their only sources of income, our young couple's savings will have to generate $124,600 in 2052. So, if they get a 5% post-retirement return, *they will need savings of $2,492,000, if they want to preserve their savings along the way.*

Our couple's ability to achieve this level of savings will depend on the growth of their income over the next 40 years. If their income stagnates at $80,000 and they average a 7% return for 40 years, an 8.5% savings plan would generate $1,360,000 for retirement. While this sounds like a great accomplishment in *today's* dollars, without a defined-benefit pension, some money from a rainy-day fund, part-time job, inheritance, income-producing business or property, or a higher return on savings, our couple would not have enough income to sustain their lifestyle in retirement.

If, however, our couple's income increases by 3% per year and they follow the same 8.5% savings plan, the amount saved each year will increase as their income does. So, our couple will get much closer to their goal. But they will still fall short. Lastly, if our couple's income grows by 4% per year, they will end up with $2,360,000. With a 5% post-retirement return, their 2052 income, including Social Security, would total $193,000. In that case, our couple would be very close to their goal of $199,600, even without other sources of income.

We are now ready to fill in Chart 12-1 for a young couple earning $80,000 in 2012.

CHART 12-1: MODEL PLAN FOR RETIRING IN 2052 WITH A 2012 INCOME OF $80,000, DIFFERENT INCOME GROWTHS, AND A 5% RETURN AFTER RETIREMENT

Income growth over next 40 years	0% Growth = Stagnant Income	3% Growth = Inflation Rate	4% Growth = Inflation + 1%
Income needed	$199,600*	$199,600*	$199,600*
Social Security	$75,000	$75,000	$75,000
Other Income	$0	$0	$0
Income needed from retirement savings	$124,600	$124,600	$124,600
Savings rate for retirement per year	6% then 7% then 8.5%	6% then 7% then 8.5%	6% then 7% then 8.5%
Retirement savings	$1,360,000	$1,760,000	$2,360,000
Income from savings	$68,000	$88,000	$118,000
Total income available	$143,000	$163,000	$193,000
Excess or shortfall in needed income	-$51,600	-$36,600	-6,600**

***Note:** If inflation averages 3% and incomes grow by 4%, $199,600 would be *less* than 77% of final pre-retirement income. But $199,600 would still sustain a reasonably good lifestyle.

****Note:** In the 4% income growth column, the shortfall of $6,600 sounds like a lot. But it is the same as $2,036 in 2012 dollars. So the numbers in this chart are not as bad as they look.

Chart 12-1 tells us three important things:

- *Pay close attention to changes in the inflation rate and your household income.* Comparing these two trends will give you a better sense of whether you are saving enough to retire on schedule or if you should adjust your savings rate.

- While the numbers in Chart 12-1 look discouraging, they show it *is* possible for young people to reach their financial goals *if* their incomes outpace inflation by roughly 1%, they have some left-over emergency funds or a little income from other sources, or they receive slightly more than 5% on their savings *after* retirement.

- Unless they have other sources of retirement income, most *young people will need to save for 40 years or longer.* This means they face a greater urgency than their parents did to start saving as early as possible.

It is important to note in this context that young people will probably be older when they retire than their parents were (or will be), because by 2052 the *minimum* age for receiving an *early* Social Security benefit will undoubtedly be higher, while the full benefit age might be 70. This might be a good thing. With a large number of people living past 90, this would re-align retirement as a 10- to 30-year period, the same as today. As a result, *people who start saving in their mid-20s could save for 45 years before retiring, while those who start in their early-30s could save for at least 40 years*. As an added bonus, the Social Security Trust Fund would not have to pay benefits to as many people for more than 30 years. Or, to paraphrase a current cliché: by 2052 "70 may be the new 65."

Most important to our topic of discussion, a later retirement age would allow more of today's modest-income Americans to save enough to retire with adequate income. However, it is worth noting that today's children are the first generation in American history to be projected to have a *shorter* life-expectancy than their parents. Ironically, if this turns out to be accurate, by 2072 we might be able (or at least want) to return to an earlier retirement age.

PLANS ACROSS THE MIDDLE-CLASS SPECTRUM

How does Chart 12-1 translate into savings plans for households earning other modest incomes? Charts 12-2A and 12-2B illustrate plans for households with 2012 incomes of $50,000, $65,000,

$95,000, and $110,000. These examples bracket the $80,000 income household in our earlier charts and cover the full range of Chapter 2's definition of modest incomes. The numbers in Chart 12-2A are based on an income growth and inflation rate of 3% per year over the next 40 years, with a post-retirement return of 5%. Chart 12-2B assumes the same inflation rate and post-retirement return, but with a pre-retirement income growth of 4% per year.

In both charts, high-income households receive larger Social Security benefits than low-income ones. However, as is the case today, high-income households will receive a *lower percentage* of retirement income from Social Security than low-income ones. So, to reach their financial goals, *high-income households will need more savings in relation to their current income than low-income ones.*

Two aspects of this odd situation warrant comment. First, a household earning $50,000 is just above the median income for the United States as reported in the 2010 census, $49,460. So, *if* we use the traditional definition of the middle-class as households in the 20%-80% range of incomes, a family earning $50,000 is marginally in the "*upper* middle class." But this does not match reality. Most families with a gross income of $50,000 qualify for the Earned Income Tax Credit and would find it difficult to sustain an 8.5% savings rate for 40 years. The same difficulty would apply to families with incomes of $65,000 if they live in expensive areas. Thus, the savings totals in Charts 12-2A and 12-2B in these two columns may be unrealistically high. Second, households with higher incomes are more likely to have other sources of retirement income such as properties and non-registered investment accounts, and should find it easier to sustain a savings rate of 8.5%. In fact, given the numbers in these charts, *families with incomes of $100,000 or more should aim for at least a 9% savings rate, with some savings going into Roth IRAs.*

CHART 12-2A: PLANS FOR RETIRING IN 2052, WITH 3% PER YEAR INCOME GROWTH RATE

2012 Income	$50,000	$65,000	$95,000	$110,000
Income needed	$130,000	$162,175	$237,025	$274,450
Social Security	$48,000	$62,500	$86,000	$96,000
Other Sources of Income	$0	$0	$0	$0
Income needed from Retirement Savings	$82,000	$100,175	$150,025	$176,450
Retirement savings rate per year	6% then 7% then 8.5%	6% then 7% then 8.5%	6% then 7% then 8.5%	6% then 7% then 8.5%
Retirement savings	$1,100,000	$1,430,000	$2,090,000	$2,420,000
Income from savings at 5% return	$55,000	$71,500	$104,500	$121,000
Total income	$103,000	$134,000	$190,500	$217,000
Shortfall or Excess of needed income	-$27,000	-$28,175	-$46,525	-$57,450

CHART 12-2B: PLANS FOR RETIRING IN 2052, WITH A 4% PER YEAR INCOME GROWTH RATE

Current Income	$50,000	$65,000	$95,000	$110,000
Income needed	$130,000	$162,175	$237,025	$274,450
Social Security	$48,000	$62,500	$86,000	$96,000
Other Sources of Income	$0	$0	$0	$0
Income needed from retirement savings	$76,750	$100,175	$150,025	$176,450
Savings rate per year	6% then 7% then 8.5%	6% then 7% then 8.5%	6% then 7% then 8.5%	6% then 7% then 8.5%
Retirement savings	$1,450,000	$1,870,500	$2,750,500	$3,170,000
Income from savings/5% return	$72,500	$93,525	$137,505	$158,500
Total income available	$120,500	$156,025	$223,505	$254,500
Excess/shortfall of income	-$9,500*	-$6,150*	-13,520*	-19,950*

***Note:** As in Chart 12-1, Chart 12-2B's "total incomes" are closer to target incomes than they appear. Even the seemingly large shortfall of $19,950 in the $110,000 column only equals $6,155 in 2012 dollars. This relatively positive outcome is the result of uniformly long savings periods, full Social Security benefits, and a 5% retirement return on savings. In earlier charts, some of our retirees took a minimum benefit, received a 4.5% return on savings, or only saved for 30 years.

The examples in Charts 12-2A and 12-2B demonstrate that saving enough to retire securely will not be easy for today's young Americans unless their incomes grow by more than inflation over the next 40 years or they have a little income from other sources. But these charts also show that with discipline, young people across the spectrum of modest-income households have a real chance to accumulate the wealth needed to eventually retire with secure and sustainable lifestyles.

✦

Before concluding this discussion, let's look at the numbers in Charts 12-2A and 12-2B from a different angle. Most young people hope to *improve* their economic situation over the next 40 years by receiving promotions or new jobs that pay significantly more than they earn now. To put this in the context of Charts 12-2A and 12-2B, instead of increasing by 3% or 4% per year, at some point in adulthood a household's income might jump from the $50,000 column to the $65,000 column. In that case, early savings would be based on the $50,000 column's savings rate while later savings would be based on the $65,000 column savings rate. As a result, even if our couple achieves a final pre-retirement income of $210,615 (equal to $65,000 in 2012 dollars) and follows the 8.5% savings plan perfectly for 40 years, they would end up with too small a nest egg to support a lifestyle similar to one costing $65,000 in 2012. But they could support a lifestyle costing more than $50,000 in 2012.

While this outcome would require a modest downward lifestyle adjustment at retirement, it is important to remember that the current fear among young people is they will *never* be able to retire or escape poverty if forced to do so. In this context, being able to sustain or modestly *improve* the lifestyle they had at age 30 or 35 would not be such a bad outcome. It is that goal that Chart 12-2B demonstrates is achievable for many households with current incomes from $50,000 to $110,000. So, contrary to what many people think, *saving is not a foolish or outdated idea.*

Or, as they say in baseball, you can't get a hit if you don't swing the bat.

CHAPTER 13

YOUR PLAN, YOUR FUTURE

Questions: What if I don't want to ever retire? What if I want to retire, but never have enough savings or income to do it?

EVEN IF YOU LOVE YOUR JOB, YOU MAY RETIRE AT SOME POINT. FOR MANY of us, this is voluntary. For others, retirement is forced on us by illness, diminished physical or mental ability, mandatory retirement age, or a job disappearing or being given to someone younger at a lower salary with less costly benefits. As a result, few people who live past age 65 keep working until they "die in the saddle." In fact, according to the Employee Benefit Research Council, *10,000 Americans retire each day.* But only 14% of adults think they will ever have enough to support a secure retirement. In other words, most Americans feel they will never be prepared for a retirement that is likely to happen to them anyway. The anxiety implied by this contrast is striking.

At the end of this chapter, you will find Chart 13-1. This is your chance to create a savings plan that will lead to a secure retirement. Before filling out Chart 13-1, gather the following information and use the charts in Chapters 11 and 12 as guides for your calculations.

First, check with the *Social Security* Administration online or at a nearby office to see what your benefits will be at various "starting" ages. While these numbers may change, especially if your income changes drastically in the future, current estimates may be used in Chart 13-1. Then, as you age, get new estimates and adjust this number on your chart.

Second, if you have a *defined-benefit pension*, estimate how much you will receive from it when you plan to retire. Some employers provide annual updates on progress toward a pension. If you belong to a union, it may also be able to provide you with projections. While these numbers are also likely to change, they may be used in Chart 13-1 as reasonable estimates.

Third, calculate the *income you will need* at retirement. For example, if your current household income is $72,000, you will need 90% of what someone with a current income of $80,000 will need. Or, if your household income is $88,000, you will need 110% of a household with an income of $80,000. So, if you plan to retire in 2052, comparing your current income to those in the charts in the last chapter should help you estimate *your* year-1 retirement income target.

If you want to retire before 2052, inflation will have less time to devalue the dollar. So, you will need less income than you would need in 2052. By studying Charts 12-1, 12-2A, and 12-2B along with the inflation chart in Chapter 4, you should be able to make a reasonable guess at the income you will need in your chosen year. If you have worked for at least 35 years, your Social Security benefit will also be slightly less than if you retired in 2052, but about the same after adjusting for inflation. If these calculations are too complex to make on your own, get help from a financial professional or use an online retirement planning calculator like the one offered by the American Association of Retired Persons (AARP).

Fourth, calculate how much *savings* you will have at retirement. If you use the plan suggested in the last two chapters and project that your savings will receive a return of 7% before retirement, you can use the numbers in Charts 12-1, 12-2A, and 12-2B to estimate the amount *you* will have after 30 or 40 years of saving. But if you change the length of time before retirement from those in the charts, be careful. For example, since savings growth accelerates over time, if you save for 35 years *your savings total will be closer to your 30-year total than your 40-year total.*

If you have a *401(k), 457, 402b, or 403B,* ask an accountant or your employer's retirement plan administrator for a projection of their worth when you plan to retire. Similarly, your stockbroker or investment advisor should be able to provide an estimate of the value of your *IRAs and non-registered investment accounts* when you reach your intended retirement age. Again, these numbers may change in the future, but they can be used as estimates in your planning.

Fifth, calculate how much *income your savings will generate* if you get a 5% rate of return *after* retirement. Mathematically, 5% = 1/20, so dividing 20 into your savings total will give your annual return from savings. If you want to use 4.5% as your return, your savings will generate 9/10 (90%) of the income you would get with a 5% return. Similarly, a 5.5% return would generate 11/10 (110%) of the income you would get with a 5% return.

And sixth, *add your income from the return on your savings, Social Security, and all other sources to get your first year retirement income.* If this is 77% of whatever income target in the last year before retirement you set for yourself, you will have a financially secure retirement. If you cannot reach that number with your planned level of saving and other sources of post-retirement income, you will have to put more money into defined contribution plans at work or IRAs and non-registered accounts at home. If you are unable to do this, you will have to wait longer to retire or accept a lower standard of living once you do so.

Lastly, remember that *your target income number is more important than any savings number.* As shown in Chart 12-1, a family with a 2012 income of $80,000 and no other income except for Social Security might need savings of $2,920,000 in 2052 to maintain their lifestyle.

But another family with the same income goal might only need $1,000,000 because they have a business, income-earning property, defined-benefit pension, or receive a significant gift or inheritance. Nevertheless, both will need the same income. In other words, focus on income goals, not a wealth goal that may not apply to you or provide enough retirement income for you.

✦

There are just a few more comments needed before you tackle Chart 13-1. First, *don't panic* if you think you will fall short with the maximum rate of savings you can manage. Keep saving and remember there are a lot of estimates in your calculations that may turn out to be inaccurate. Social Security may pay more or less. Your savings may grow more or less than expected, both before and after retirement. Your pre-retirement income might increase more or less than you expect. Inflation might be lower or higher. Taxes and health costs may change to your advantage or disadvantage. These are the variables that made saving over the *last* 40 years more effective than many in my generation guessed it would be. Those who kept saving have ended up well. Many who didn't are now in trouble. In short, *there is nothing to be gained by giving up, and much to be gained by starting a savings plan and then sticking with it.*

Second, no matter how good your estimates are, you will have to adjust them in coming years. This is what I did with my annual reviews. Re-doing Chart 13-1 every one or two years will help you adjust your current spending and savings habits, correct past assumptions where necessary, and come up with more accurate target income and savings goals.

Third, given the uncertainty associated with any projections, you might set your target retirement income slightly higher than you project you will really need *or* lower your pre-retirement return estimate. If nothing else, these pessimistic projections will motivate you to meet or surpass your savings goal each year. This is what I did in my annual reviews. I assumed reasonable minimums for all positive factors and reasonable maximums for negative ones, thereby allowing for a 5% margin of error in case my "true" projections were too optimistic. As it turned out, my wife and I consistently exceeded my projections, in some five year periods by a wide margin. However, this changed in the eight years before I retired, 2001 to 2009, a period that included the post-9/11 economic slowdown and the recession of 2007-2009. Happily, in the end, the growth of our savings over 35 years almost perfectly matched my earliest projections.

✦

It is time to put your numbers on Chart 13-1. Take out a pad and pencil or a calculator (as a retired teacher of math I prefer the former). Do some arithmetic. Then fill in Chart 13-1. Pick the column that best describes how long you will save by the year you intend to retire and whether you will be at minimum or full Social Security age (or somewhere in between) by that date. *You only have to fill in one column, unless you want to compare two possibilities*. If necessary, use an online retirement calculator or ask a financial professional to help you or to review your work. But remember that *this is your plan. You are responsible for putting it into practice, limiting spending and debt, saving every year, keeping track of your plan, and making adjustments to it as needed.*

CHART 13-1: SAVINGS PLANS FOR RETIRING BETWEEN 2042 AND 2052, OR SOON AFTER

Age of Retirement and years until that age	Minimum Social Security Age/ after 30 years saving	Minimum Social Security Age/ after 40 years saving	Full Social Security Benefit age/after 30 years saving	Full Social Security Benefit age/after 40 years saving
Income needed				
Social Security				
Other Sources of Income				
Total Income Needed				
Retirement savings rate per year				
Total savings				
Income from savings, at 5% return				
Total income available				
Excess or shortfall of needed income				

Congratulations! You now have a savings plan that will get you to retirement. In the next chapter we will discuss what happens *after* you retire. After all, *getting to retirement is not the end of our story*. It is just the beginning of a new and hopefully long period of your life.

To put the theme of this chapter as succinctly as possible, pick a date to retire and save as much as you can before then. Be flexible about pushing back this date, but don't keep putting retirement off because you would like to be richer. Too many people wait until they are too old to have a productive or enjoyable retirement. Some wait so long they develop a debilitating disease or die while they are still working or just after retiring. In other words, *while it is important to do all you can to create a financially secure future, it makes no sense to end up with lots of money and no future at all*. Retirement can be an interesting, enjoyable, and lengthy period of life. But first you have to let it begin.

CHAPTER 14

RETIREMENT, THE FINAL FRONTIER

Avoiding the urge to outlive your money

Questions: Now that I'm retired, what do I do with myself? How can I know how much I should take as distributions each year? Is an annuity right for me? How about a reverse mortgage? How do I figure out how to use up my money so it will last until my spouse and I die?

THE DAY YOU RETIRE MAY SEEM LIKE THE FINISH LINE IN THE RACE OF life. You may have worked for 40 years or longer, paid for a house that you now own "mortgage-free," raised children, helped put them through school, and seen them become adults with lives of their own. Now is the time to enjoy the fruits of your labors. You can focus your time and energy on hobbies or recreation, devoting your money to your and your spouse's needs and wants instead of spending much of it on others. With many of the hard jobs of life behind you, both financially and emotionally, you can do what you want *within your means* for the rest of "your remaining days."

As appealing as this picture may be, it rarely matches reality. If you are lucky, retirement lasts 20 to 30 years, longer than childhood and in some cases almost as long as the income-earning period of adulthood. So *retirement is not about your "remaining days."* In fact, given the time left to most people, it is important to remain physically, mentally, and socially active. It also helps if you find ways to contribute your talents and skills to others or to organizations that are important to you. In other words, *it is best to see this time not as one of unbroken recreation and rest, but as a time in which you have the freedom to reinvent yourself (a second adolescence?) by facing new challenges and having new adventures.* Thus, while retirement should *not* be seen as a time to totally avoid stress or life's demands, the good news is you may now be the one placing demands and stresses upon yourself rather than having them thrust on you by others.

It is equally important to *continue to budget and plan financially.* With no way to get large amounts of new money, retirees have to manage their investments, plan for new expenses (above all, medical ones), decide about distributions from savings, and keep tabs on the effect of inflation on living costs. Luckily, for many people, playing a greater role in managing their own financial affairs is an enjoyable and mentally rewarding part of retirement. It is for me.

The most important aspects of post-retirement financial planning are judging the adequacy of your income each year and arranging to receive money from your investments in a way that preserves as much of your savings as possible while taking maximum advantage of tax laws. Accordingly, it helps to re-structure your savings to emphasize investments that generate lots of *dividends*. This minimizes the need to sell investments to pay for living expenses.

RETIREMENT OPTIONS: USES FOR MONEY

If you have enough income to sustain your desired lifestyle forever, take what you need from savings, Social Security, and other sources of income. Then manage your investments so they will be preserved with moderate growth. And make sure your Will designates heirs who will get your "left-over" money when you die. But for anyone who is *not* confident they will have enough income, there are major decisions to make. Should you get a part-time job? Should you purchase an annuity or reverse mortgage? If so, what kinds? Should you take distributions that outstrip the return on your investments? If so, when will your savings disappear? Should you move to a less costly home or apartment? For those living in high-tax states, should you move to a state with lower taxes, and perhaps better weather? Lastly, if you have just enough money to maintain your current lifestyle, do you want to "take" more from savings to support a more expensive lifestyle?

These choices involve deeper questions about your values. Do you want to leave inheritances to descendants or charities? Or, do you see your estate as solely existing to support you and your spouse or partner for the rest of your lives? Do you want to financially help grandchildren and children while you are alive? If so, what kind of help? Would you provide money for a child's business or house, supplement a child's income, pay medical bills, buy a car for a grandchild or child, pay for a grandchild's education, or bail a child out of a credit crisis or the consequences of alcoholism, drug addiction, or crime? Lastly, do you want or need to provide for your parents in *their* old age? If you would like to provide for family members in any of these ways, consult an attorney to discuss gifting or the setting up of Trusts. But be careful. It is bad enough if you drain your resources to support your own lifestyle and end up with no money. It is worse if you run out of money because you disregarded your own needs to meet the financial needs of others.

Just before *and* after retiring, you and your spouse or partner should discuss these questions and come up with *mutually* agreed-upon answers to them. You should also *update your "end of life" documents (Living Wills, Health Proxies, Powers of Attorney, Wills)*. Hopefully, you have been doing this regularly. But this is especially important after retirement. After all, it is only realistic to prepare for you or your spouse becoming physically or mentally incapacitated, one of you dying, your children's lives changing (marriages, new children, divorces), or your estate growing or shrinking. After retirement, whenever there are big changes in your life or finances, you should review these documents immediately to see if they still fit your situation.

Discussing these documents will also shape the way you handle your finances. Interestingly, in a recent insurance industry study *70% of baby boomers said having an enjoyable retirement is more important than leaving an inheritance to children*. So, most feel it would be okay to use up their savings, as long as they do so in a way that ensures the money lasts until the end of their lives. In a related question, *86% said they feel an obligation to have enough savings to be self-sufficient until the end of their lives*. Some even said this is the greatest gift they could give their children. After all, financially self-sufficient parents don't drain their children's financial resources.

Once you have answered these questions in a way that fits *your* values, stay on top of the financial decisions needed to use your estate in the way you want. If necessary, live on less for a couple of years to stay on track. Make changes in your investments as needed. And, if possible, maintain a margin of error in your savings in case there are sudden dips in the stock market or increases in inflation or your expenses. If any of these things happen and you just keep doing what you have always done, your financial problems will not go away. They will grow worse. So, *adjust as quickly as possible*. In the long run, this will give you the best chance to solve financial problems that arise.

INVADING PRINCIPAL WITHOUT THROWING CAUTION TO THE WIND

What happens if you get to retirement and don't have enough savings? Or, if you are forced to retire by illness to you or a loved one for whom you are the sole care-giver or because you are let go from your job before reaching your pension or savings goals? Depending on circumstances, there are several ways to handle these situations.

If you are healthy, you could search for a job in your field or a related field. If this fails, you could get a full- or part-time job in retail or a service industry. This is where most jobs are available for older workers today. While these jobs are usually low-paying, they can supplement the income generated from savings and other sources. If your earned income is less than the maximum amount allowed by Social Security, you could start taking Social Security as soon as you qualify for an early benefit. Or, if you are at or beyond full benefit age, you could earn any amount and draw Social Security. Getting a job might also give you time to take smaller distributions from savings, which would allow them to grow and get closer to your savings goal. But remember, the time will come when you will no longer be able to work. And it might come sooner than you would like.

If you are close to your savings target and your health makes it impossible to get a job or you don't want to do this, you could cut back on expenses for a few years in order to reach your savings goal for later years. Doing this takes discipline and some research. But it is amazing how much you can save if you look for bargains in all aspects of spending. To cite just a few examples, online pharmacies may cut prescription co-pays to a quarter of what you pay at local pharmacies. You could cut back on cable television and telephone costs. You could pay closer attention to how often and where you eat out. Or you could buy a reverse mortgage, although, as I have already said, I do not think this is a good choice.

No matter how desperate you are to have more income, *resist the urge to increase the riskiness of your investments in an effort to get a higher return* on savings. This tactic will expose you to an increased possibility of suffering a sudden decline in savings, with little or no time to recover. However, you *could* decide to take distributions that are larger than the return on your savings. If you choose this strategy, *first* calculate how much your savings will shrink as a result of your intended distributions. Online retirement planning sites can help with this calculation. Or, you could consult a financial planner, many of whom call this option "*invading your principal.*" Moreover, if you don't project how long your money will last, you may end up with no income other than Social Security. Finally, you could ask for financial help from siblings, children, other relatives, or friends. This, of course, assumes you are willing to "swallow your pride" and that anyone is able and willing to offer this support.

FORCED DISTRIBUTIONS: IN OLD AGE AND BEYOND

No matter how well you arrange things when you first retire, *our tax laws eventually force you to use up the wealth you have in tax-deferred accounts*. These rules are based on a simple premise. The government has allowed you to put off paying tax on some of your income *and* the growth of some of your savings for many years. But the government has no interest in allowing you or your heirs to put off paying taxes forever. In short, *these retirement accounts defer taxes, they don't avoid them*. Consequently, when you reach 70½ you are no longer allowed to make contributions to and must take distributions from all retirement accounts except Roth-IRAs. The amount of this *Required Mandatory Distribution, or RMD,* is determined by three actuarial tables the IRS uses to calculate the *maximum* number of years you and your spouse are likely to live. For example, at age 70½ the IRS might set your and your spouse's collective life expectancy at 26 years (age 96 ½), even though *individual* life-expectancy at 70½ is roughly 16 years for a man and 18 years for a woman. This calculation creates an RMD of $3,650 for every $100,000 in tax-deferred savings, a distribution rate of 3.65%. *You may take more, but you cannot take less without paying a penalty*. Most important, *income tax must be paid on RMDs*.

In each following year, the IRS re-figures your collective life-expectancy and your RMD increases to a higher percentage of the money left in your tax-deferred accounts, which also increases your income tax bill. *Within a very few years, the RMD outstrips any return you could receive and your principal begins to shrink.* Then, as each year passes, this shrinkage accelerates. Finally, for the few who live long enough to reach the end of the IRS's actuarial charts, at age 106 the RMD is 50% of all money left in tax-deferred accounts, with the remainder taken as a final distribution the following year. Hence, RMDs are meant to ensure the federal government gets at least some of the deferred taxes due to it before the owner of tax-deferred accounts dies. Meanwhile, *Roth-IRAs, non-registered savings, and other assets are exempt from RMDs*. So people with these resources may retain or grow this part of their estate past age 70½.

INHERITING TAX DEFERRED ACCOUNTS

If you die *after* 70½ but *before* using up your tax-deferred money, the beneficiaries named in your account documents may dissolve your accounts and pay all income tax owed according to their own income tax rate in the year of the inheritance. Or, if your beneficiaries are your spouse, children, or grandchildren, they may change the title of your retirement accounts to their names. In this case, they must continue to take the RMDs *you* would have taken if you were still alive, paying tax on that money each year according to their own tax bracket. But this spreads out the tax burden over many years. At the same time, inherited Roth-IRAs must be rolled over into regular IRAs in the name of the beneficiary, making them subject to the same rules as apply to inherited tax-deferred accounts. This means your retirement savings, but not necessarily your other savings or assets, will be completely used up by your heirs in the year *you* would have turned 107 (at the latest). However, getting this money will supplement their income, which should make it easier for them to put money into their own savings plans and IRAs along the way.

If you are *not* yet 70½ when you die and your RMDs have not started, a beneficiary has several additional options. If he or she does nothing, income taxes must be paid on all the money in inherited tax-deferred accounts in the year of your death. But if the beneficiary is the spouse of the deceased, he or she may re-name the inherited account as a "*Spousal IRA*" in his or her own name. This moves the RMD to an actuarial table based on the surviving spouse's age, a significant benefit if the surviving spouse is younger than the deceased.

If the beneficiaries are children or other individuals, they may choose to spread out distributions and the resultant tax load over a five year period. Or, as a last option, they may roll over inherited IRAs into a "*Stretch IRA*" in their own name. While RMDs must be taken from a Stretch IRA immediately, they are based on *the heir's* life-expectancy. As a result, the amounts are smaller and the tax-deferral lasts much longer. This is the best option for younger generation heirs.

In all cases, the lesson here is simple: if your savings are mostly in retirement accounts and you live a long life, *the size of your estate will shrink toward the end of your life.* For those who are at the upper end of the modest-income range and beyond, the increased income from RMDs may create a tax load that quickly lowers net income enough to become a problem. Moreover, *once you die, the proceeds from your estate will continue to shrink* because of taxes your heirs will have to pay on your savings. And all of this is in addition to any estate taxes that might be due at the time of your death, a factor that is rarely significant for modest-income people.

INVADING YOUR PRINCIPAL FOR SUN AND FUN

Some retirees have enough savings to maintain their lifestyle without invading principal but *choose* to do so anyway to have a more enjoyable lifestyle. If you want to do this, do the same calculation as someone who plans to use up savings because they have not reached their savings target, making sure you know how much money you can take annually without running out of money before you and your spouse die. If you are unsure how to do this, get help from a financial planner or an online retirement planning site. While this can be complicated, we will end by projecting how long a couple's money would last if they take distributions that outstrip their return, starting voluntarily before age 70½ and continuing once RMDs force them to take larger and larger distributions. Each example relates to a household with a 2012 pre-retirement income of $80,000.

Let's begin with a 62-year-old couple who retire in 2012 and consider two choices. In the first, they use all of their year-1 retirement income without contributing any money to savings. Then they maintain the same lifestyle in following years. As inflation erodes the value of the dollar, this forces them to increase their income and invade their principal. If a couple chooses this option, averages a 5% return after retirement, and then faces RMDs, they will run out of money in 22 years, with only Social Security after that. So they will be poverty-stricken by age 84. Of course, if they get less than a 5% return or have less saved money, they will run out of money sooner.

Whether this is long enough depends on how long you expect to live or in fact do live. For example, given the longevity of my wife's and my parents, all of whom have made it to at least age 89, with three already having lived past 90, we did not consider 22 years long enough. When I planned our retirement, I set a goal of having financial resources left when my wife reaches 98 (I would be 104)! Of course, in all likelihood, this means we will leave inheritances.

In the second scenario, a 62-year-old couple uses their entire income *plus* $10,000 in year-1 of retirement to live a higher lifestyle, a lifestyle they continue in future years despite the effects of inflation and RMDs. In this case, again with a 5% return, they run out of money in about 17 years. For most people, this is too short a period. After all, as noted earlier, the *average* retiree today lives 16½ years. And many of us hope to be (and will be) "above average" in this regard.

If we examine the same choices for a young couple that will retire in 2052, we get a worse result due to the lower percentage of income provided by Social Security and the resultant need to draw more from savings. If this couple uses all of their year-1 retirement income without contributing to savings, and then maintains the same lifestyle in following years, they will run out of money in slightly less than 20 years. And, if they use all of their income *plus* an extra $32,400 in the first year of retirement, the same as $10,000 in 2012, and continue to live the same lifestyle in following years, they will run out of money in just under 15 years.

The numbers in these four examples are unlikely to match your situation. And they don't match mine. As pointed out in the Preface, these examples are only meant to illustrate the concept under discussion. So *do your own calculations before taking distributions that are larger than your return on savings*. You should also create annual benchmarks that will help you keep track of the pace at which your money is disappearing. Lastly, ask a financial professional to monitor your progress, especially as you age and begin to lose some financial management skills. If you decide to take larger-than-return distributions, you don't want any surprises 10 or 20 years later.

Nevertheless, it is not crazy or selfish to invade your principal. As the old saying goes, "you can't take it with you." And your children did not earn or save this money. Nor, are they *entitled* to it. If they get an inheritance, they should feel lucky and appreciative. If they don't, they shouldn't feel that something that *belonged* to them was taken away, either because you used it up or gave it to charity. *Giving an inheritance to descendants is a kindness, not an obligation.*

Just *be careful you don't outlive your money*. If that happens, you will become dependent on the government or your children. That is why it is important to develop and follow a *life plan and a financial plan* that will get you to retirement and then give you the best chance to remain financially self-sufficient to the end of your life.

✦

If I could leave you with one last piece of advice, it would be this. Research and carefully think out every major *lifestyle and financial* decision you make throughout adulthood. This applies to buying insurance, paying taxes, acquiring a car, purchasing or renting a place to live, getting an education, handling credit and debt, and investing money. If you do this consistently, you are likely to find the best solutions to problems that arise along the way. If you don't, you will make a lot of impulsive choices. You are also likely to fall into debt and short of your savings goals. In fact, while it is always good to gather expert opinions from books, magazine articles, and people like accountants, stockbrokers, insurance agents, realtors, or financial planners, relying on their advice alone is not the best way to manage your life. It is far better to *become as informed as possible and manage your own affairs*. In short, the examined life is more likely to end up as a financially successful life. As an added bonus, examining your life can be fun and interesting.

Above all, remember that the goal of any life plan is to live a full and good life. Having money throughout adulthood and in retirement is just one means toward that end. It is worthy of your best efforts. But it is not the goal. Nor should it determine every choice you make in life. In short, *your first goal is to "live well." Your second goal is to "save for life" to make it possible to live well for as long as needed.*

To put the central message of this book as succinctly as possible, I can do no better than to quote the TV show Star Trek: "*go forth and prosper*."

Yes, I am a baby boomer.

The End

GLOSSARY: KEY WORDS AND PHRASES FROM THE TEXT

—a—

Adjusted gross income: Income of a tax filer after taking personal deductions, but before capital gains, other deductions, and credits are subtracted from income.

After-tax dollars: Money left after all taxes are paid.

Alternative Minimum Tax (AMT): System for calculating income taxes owed by high-earning taxpayers. This calculation is compared to tax owed using tax brackets, deductions, and credits.

Amortization: Method used to calculate monthly payments and total amount due on a mortgage.

Annuity: Financial product purchased with savings. The holder of an annuity receives income for the rest of his/her life. There are many types of annuities, including ones with fixed pay-outs, pay-outs that grow over time, and options to buy back money or convert some of the annuity amount into a death benefit.

APR (actual percentage rate): The rate of interest paid on a loan or mortgage when all interest, fees, and other charges are calculated as an annual percentage of the principal borrowed.

Assets: Money, property, and investments a person, household, organization, or corporation "owns." If all debts and other liabilities are subtracted from this amount, the result is called "net assets."

—b—

Balloon payment: Amount paid at the end of a loan or mortgage that is larger than previous payments.

Bear market: A stock market when it is consistently losing value (going down).

Before-tax dollars: Income or other resources before any taxes are paid on those amounts.

Benchmark: Prediction of financial goal to be attained at a specific time in the future. When a benchmark is compared to actual performance, individuals can see if they are on track to fulfill their financial plan.

Beneficiary: Person named in a Will, Trust, or insurance policy who will receive assets or income derived from those assets immediately, at a specified time in the future, or at the death of the asset owner.

Benefit: Health insurance, pension, life insurance, or savings plan given to an employee beyond salary or wage. Benefits should be considered part of an employee's total compensation.

Budget: Document used to plan and track income and spending.

Bull market: A stock market that is consistently gaining in value (going up).

—c—

Capital gain: Increase in value of an investment or property from when it was bought to when it is sold.

Capital loss: Loss of value in an investment or property from when it was bought to when it is sold.

Cash value: Money built up within a life insurance policy savings account from premium payments.

Closing costs: Fees paid up-front to a financial company when a mortgage is signed. These fees do not count as a down payment because they do not reduce the principal of the mortgage.

Compound interest: Interest paid on the combination of principal and previous interest. Compound interest is charged on debts or earned on invested money.

Contribution: Money put into a retirement investment account or pension plan.

Co-payment (co-pay): Amount paid by a patient when medical services are used. Co-pays qualify that expense for partial or total health insurance payment of the rest of the bill.

Cost basis: Amount paid for an asset in the past plus capital improvements to that asset. This is compared to the amount received when the asset is sold to calculate capital gains tax that must be paid.

Cost-of-living adjustment (COLA): Increase built into a rental agreement, employment contract, or pension plan based on increases in the cost of living in the future.

Credit: 1. Borrowed money. 2. The financial system for creating/managing debt.

Credit score: Rating of a consumer's financial health and history used by financial companies to decide if they should give that consumer a loan or mortgage and, if so, at what interest rate.

—d—

Death benefit: Money paid to beneficiaries upon the death of a person by an insurance policy.

Deductible: Money paid by an insured individual before insurance payments "kick in" for an expense covered in the policy. Deductibles are most common in health, home, and vehicle insurance policies.

Deduction: Amount subtracted from a tax filer's gross or adjusted gross income. Some deductions are standard, while others require a listing (itemization) of specific costs for that expense category.

Deferred compensation (benefit): Money or benefits earned now to be paid to an employee at a later date.

Defined-benefit pension: Pension plan with a set amount to be paid when a person retires. These plans are managed by the employer or his/her agent.

Defined-contribution pension: Pension plan with limits of how much can be contributed by an employee and/or the employer on an annual basis. Money in these plans is managed by the employee and grows or shrinks depending on the return investments earn.

Deflation: Period when cost-of-living and prices are dropping.

Dependent: Person who is the financial responsibility of another person.

Depreciation: Loss of worth of an object (tool, building, equipment, etc.), as it is used. Depreciation is commonly used to determine the amount of a tax deduction as a business or personal expense.

Disability insurance: Insurance that gives money to an individual who is unable to work or earn a living.

Disclaimer Trust: Trust set up by an heir after the death of an individual who owned assets. The heir "disclaims" part of his/her inheritance by placing assets in a Trust to minimize taxes that will have to be paid later, usually by children or grandchildren.

Disposable income: Income left after all basic needs (housing, food, medical expenses, taxes, etc.) are met.

Distribution: Money taken from a retirement account as income.

Diversification: Practice of investing in a wide range of financial instruments, sectors of the economy, and other assets. This minimizes the risk associated with any one investment.

Dividend: Pre-set payment corporations make to owners of their stock.

Down payment: Partial payment for a purchase, loan, or mortgage made "up front," with the rest of the purchase cost to be paid later, usually with interest.

—e—

Earned Income Tax Credit (EITC): Tax credit given to low-income taxpayers who have earned income, thereby lowering the amount of federal income tax owed.

Effective Interest Rate: Interest rate paid on a debt after tax savings are taken into account.

Elimination Period: Time between the onset of long-term care or disability before payments begin from an insurance policy.

Estate: Assets owned by an individual, usually in reference to amounts left to heirs in a Will or Trust(s).

Estate tax: Tax due at time of death on money, property, and other assets inherited by heirs.

—f—

Federal Reserve Bank ("the Fed"): Independent branch of U.S. government that sets monetary policies, such as the amount of money in circulation and interest rates for borrowing by governments and banks.

Fixed-rate loan: Loan (particularly student loan or mortgage) with an interest rate that is guaranteed not to change over the course of the loan's term.

Foreclosure: Early termination of a mortgage by a financial company due to the homeowner's inability or unwillingness to make mortgage payments.

—g, h—

Gift: Assets given by one person to another without expectation of repayment.

Gross income: Total income made by an individual or household from all sources.

Health Proxy: Document that gives another individual authority to make health care decisions for a person when or if that person is no longer able to make decisions about these matters.

Heir: Person who inherits money, property, or other assets from another person.

Home equity: Part of a home's value that is owned by the homeowner as a result of having made a down payment, paid back part of the principal in a mortgage, or growth in the value of the home.

Home equity loan: Money borrowed against home equity. The homeowner regains the home equity when the loan is paid back.

Hyperinflation: Period of extreme increase in the cost-of-living or the price of specific goods and services.

—i—

Income: Amount of money made by an individual, household, corporation, or government.

Individual Retirement Accounts (IRAs): Investment accounts designed to accumulate and grow money for retirement.

Inflation: Increase in cost-of-living or price of goods and services.

Inflation-adjusted income: Measure used to compare the buying power of two incomes at different times after the effect of inflation in the intervening years is included in the comparison.

Inheritance: 1. Act of receiving assets from someone after his/her death. 2. Assets received as an heir or beneficiary under someone else's Will.

Intestate: Dying without a Will.

Interest: 1. Money paid on a loan as a percentage of the principal borrowed. 2. Money paid to an investor as a percentage of the amount that was invested.

Interest-only loan: Loan in which payments only cover the interest owed.

Invading principal: Taking distributions from savings that are greater than the return those savings earn. Over time, this reduces the amount of one's savings.

Itemized deduction: Deduction taken to reduce a person's or household's taxable income based on a list of actual expenditures for a particular category of spending.

—j, k, l, m—

Lifestyle: The way a person or household lives, including the way money is spent.

Liquidity: Ability to turn investments or other property into cash quickly.

Living Will: Document that spells out how a person would like to be treated, or not treated, medically if he/she becomes incapable of making such decisions or expressing his/her desires.

Long-term care insurance: Insurance that pays for long-term medical care in a nursing home, senior living facility, or at home for a defined period. Covers expenses not covered by health insurance.

Lump-sum buy out: Money given to a person at retirement or dismissal from his/her employment with no further money or pension due later.

Means: Money or resources possessed by or available to a person or household.

Medicaid: Government-sponsored health care program for low-income Americans of all ages.

Medicare: Government-sponsored health care program for senior Americans at all income levels.

Medicare tax: Money paid into the federal government's Medicare Trust Fund by employees and their employers to pay for Medicare benefits received by seniors.

Middle class: Segment of population that falls in between those considered poor and rich in terms of income and/or wealth.

Mortgage: Loan taken out to pay for a home or other real property.

—n, o, p—

Net income: Income left after all taxes are subtracted.

Net worth: Wealth held by an individual or household after debts and other liabilities are subtracted.

Non-registered (unregistered) savings: Investments and other savings accounts that are not registered with the government and therefore do not receive special tax benefits.

Overdraft: Money withdrawn from a bank account that is greater than the amount in that account.

Pension: Money paid by a company or government agency to an individual after retirement.

Personal deduction: Standard deduction from gross income for each person claimed by a tax filer.

Post-retirement income: Amount of individual or household income after retirement.

Power of attorney: Document giving other individual(s) the right to manage a person's affairs and make legal and financial decisions in the event he/she is not able or competent to do this for him/herself.

Pre-existing medical condition: Health issue that existed before a health insurance policy went into effect.

Premium: Periodic payment to an insurance company that ensures a policy stays in force.

Pre-retirement income: Individual or household income in the years before retirement.

Pre-tax dollars: Money, such as income, before any tax is paid on it.

Primary residence: Home or rental unit that an individual or family lives in most of the year.

Prime Interest Rate (the Prime): Interest rate set by the Federal Reserve Bank for borrowing by banks and governments. Interest rates on consumer debt and interest paid to bond-holders by governments and companies are set in relation to the Prime.

Principal: 1. Amount of money borrowed in a loan or mortgage. 2. Money held in savings or investment accounts that may earn interest or dividends. Principal may grow or shrink over time.

Probate: Process overseen by a state Probate Judge by which a Will is approved and used to dispense assets held by and responsibilities of the deceased individual.

—q, r—

Refinancing ("re-fi"): Getting a new mortgage at a lower interest rate to replace an old mortgage before it is fully paid back.

Required Mandatory Distribution (RMD): Money a senior is

required to take as a distribution from his/her tax-deferred retirement accounts. RMDs start at age 70½ and increase after that.

Residual value: Amount that will have to be paid to buy a leased vehicle at the end of the lease.

Retirement incentive: Money or benefits given to an employee to encourage him/her to retire immediately.

Return (on investment): Money made from interest, dividends, and growth of an investment, usually calculated as a percentage of the total value of the investment on an annual basis.

Reverse mortgage: Agreement to sell equity in a home to a financial company in exchange for a monthly or annual payment to the homeowner for as long as he/she lives in the house or until death.

Risk: Level of uncertainty in the future value of an investment (property, stock, mutual fund, etc.).

Roth IRA: Retirement investment account in which taxes are paid up front on contributions, with no taxes paid later on growth in the account or distributions as long as they are taken after age 59½.

—S—

Savings: Money put aside for future use.

Savings rate: Percentage of annual gross income an individual or household puts aside in savings.

Second mortgage: Mortgage written on a property or home that already has an existing mortgage.

Short sale: Selling a house for less than the principal still owed in an existing mortgage.

Simple interest: Interest calculated as a percentage of the original amount of money owed or saved. Interest is not paid on earlier interest added to the debt or asset.

Simplified Employee Pension Plan (SEP-IRA): Retirement account set up and managed by an employee but funded by his/her employer. Self-employed people may do both for themselves.

Social Security: Government guaranteed income program for seniors and disabled individuals who paid into the system while they worked.

Social Security Tax: Money paid into the Social Security Trust Fund by employees and employers.

Spousal benefit: Social Security pension available for non-qualifying spouses of seniors who have qualified for Social Security benefit pensions.

Stagflation: Period when the economy is stagnant (shrinking or not growing) but prices are rising.

Standard deduction: Amount deducted for a specific category of spending from gross adjusted income without listing actual expenditures for that category of spending.

Sub-prime (interest): Interest charged on a loan that is less than the Prime Rate set by the Federal Reserve Bank.

—t—

Taxable Income: Income left after all deductions, credits, and capital gains income is subtracted from a tax filer's gross income. Taxable income determines the marginal tax bracket of a person or household.

Tax bracket (marginal): Range of income subject to a specific percentage to be paid as income tax.

Tax Credit: Amount subtracted directly from the amount of tax due on a person's or household's income for a specific expense or category of spending.

Tax-deferred (account): Retirement account in which tax is not paid until money is removed from the account after age 59½.

Tax filer: Individual who files a tax return with the Internal Revenue Service or a state's tax agency.

Tax load: Total amount paid by an individual or household including government fees and federal, state, and local taxes, sometimes expressed as a percentage of gross income.

Term: Length of time associated with a loan, mortgage, or insurance policy.

Term Life Insurance: Life insurance that is rented for a specific term.

Title: Document stating ownership of an asset (house, property, car, etc.).

Transferability: Ability to move money or assets from the ownership or use of one individual to another.

Trust: Financial instrument that sets aside assets for use by certain individuals now and in the future. Trusts may be established to protect assets from being mishandled or squandered by a beneficiary or to minimize estate taxes or the tax burden of future beneficiaries of the Trust.

Trustee: Individual named to manage a Trust and see that its instructions are followed.

—u, v, w, x, y, z—

Underwater: Condition in which the remaining principal on an existing mortgage is more than the home is worth. This condition is also called being "upside-down."

Unemployment Insurance: Government program to give temporary income to unemployed individuals who have paid into the program when they worked.

Unemployment Tax: Tax paid to the federal government by income earners and their employers to pay for Unemployment Insurance benefits.

Variable-rate loan: Loan (particularly student loan or mortgage) with an interest rate that may change over time, depending on changes in the Prime Rate set by the Federal Reserve Bank.

Wealth: All net assets (net worth) a person or household possesses.

Will: Legal document spelling out how a person wants his/her assets to be distributed upon death. A Will may also name individuals to act as Executors of the estate left in the Will and individuals who will care for dependents (especially minor children) of the deceased.

Whole life insurance: Insurance policy that includes both a death benefit and a savings component. There are several versions of these policies (whole life, universal life, and variable life), depending on the range of investments the insurance company is allowed to hold within the policy.

Wrap-around policy: Whole life policy purchased in advance by someone with an existing term life policy to replace that policy when the term life policy can no longer be renewed.

CPSIA information can be obtained at www.ICGtesting.com
Printed in the USA
BVOW06s1313240615

405996BV00003B/6/P

9 780990 947400